# SCIENCE CONNECTIONS 2

Jane Taylor

Arthur Harwood

Rebecca Smith

Ian Pritchard

Lyn Nicholls

Collins Educational

*An Imprint of* HarperCollins*Publishers*

Published by Collins Educational
An imprint of HarperCollins Publishers Ltd
77-85 Fulham Palace Road
London
W6 8JB

First published 1998

ISBN 000 327863 8

Jane Taylor, Arthur Harwood, Rebecca Smith, Ian Pritchard and Lyn Nicholls assert the moral right to be identified as the authors of this work.

British Library Cataloguing in Publication Data
A catalogue record for this book is available from the British Library.

Edited by Helen Parr

Design and illustrations by Visual Image, Taunton Somerset

Cover design by Chi Leung

Picture research by Cathy Blackie

Production by James Graves

Printed and bound by Scotprint Ltd, Musselburgh

## Acknowledgements

cover: Bruce Coleman Ltd/Jeff Foott Productions

Inset: Bruce Coleman Ltd/Jane Burton

p1 Zefa; p4 Natural History Photo Agency/Moira Savomus; p5 Biophoto Associates; p6 (top left) Biophoto Associates; p5 (top right) Science Photo Library/Andrew Syred; p6 (top middle) Science Photo Library/Bruce Iverson; p7 Science Photo Library/Andrew Syred; p8 Science Photo Library/Dr Jeremy Burgess; p10 Bruce Coleman Ltd/CS Nielsen; p11 Harry Smith; p12 (top) Biophoto Associates; p12 (bottom) Science Photo Library/Andrew Syred; p13 British Library Reproductions; p15 Kobal Collection/The Black Hole, Walt Disney; p16 (both) Mary Evans Picture Library; p17 (top left) Ancient Art and Architecture/Ronald Sheridan; p17 (top right) Science Photo Library; p17 (bottom) Science Photo Library/NASA/ JISAS; p20 Science Photo Library/MSSSO, ANU; p21 (left) Science Photo Library/David Parker; p21 (right) Science Photo Library/ Frank Sullo; p22 (top) BBC Publicity; p22 (middle) Science Photo Library/M-SAT Ltd; p23 Science Photo Library/NASA; p24 Science Photo Library/NASA; p25 Bruce Coleman Ltd/CC Lockwood; p27 Science Photo Library/David Nunuk; p28 Science Photo Library/JL Charmet; p29 Science Photo Library/NASA; p31 Collections/John Wender; p32 Collections/John Potts; p33 (left and right middle) Biophoto Associates; p33 (middle middle) Geoscience Features; p33 (left and middle bottom) Bruce Coleman Ltd/Jane Bolton; p33 (upper bottom) Rex Features; p 33 (right bottom) Zefa; p34 Bruce Coleman Ltd/David Austen; p35 (left) Biophoto Associates; p35 (right) Collections/Michael Diggin; p36 Robert Harding Picture

Library; p37 Biophoto Associates; p38 Hutchison Library/Catherine Blackie; p39 Science Photo Library/Institute of Oceanography/ NERC; p40 Image Bank/P & G Bowater; p42 Bruce Coleman Ltd/Jules Cowan; p43 Collections/Robin Weaver; p43 Topham Picturepost/Louisa Buller; p46 (left) Rex Features/Brian Rasic; p46 (middle) Zefa; p46 (bottom) Hutchison Library; p48 Hutchison Library; p49 (top) Hutchison Library; p49 (bottom) Rex Features/Philippe Hurlin; p50 Bruce Coleman Ltd/William S Paton; p52 Bruce Coleman Ltd/Kim Taylor; p53 Format/Sally Lancaster; p55 Mary Evans Picture Library; p56 (top) CEL Instruments; p56 (middle) Zefa/Hemlinger; p57 (top) Bruce Coleman Ltd/Konrad Wolte; p57 Bruce Coleman Ltd/Sir Jeremy Grayson; p59 Rex Features/Steve Nicholson; p60 (top) Bruce Coleman Ltd/Leonard Lee Rue III; p60 (left middle) Rex Features; p60 (right middle) Bruce Coleman Ltd/Kim Taylor; p63 Science Photo Library/PM Motta & S Makubo; p65 Rex Features; p67 Wellcome Institute Library; p69 Rex Features/Robin Kerr; p70 Robert Harding Picture Library/Adam Wolfitt; p71 (top) Science Photo Library/Dr Jeremy Burgess; p71 (left) Bruce Coleman Ltd/Michael Fogden; p71 (right) Science Photo Library/Dr Jeremy Burgess; p72 Science Photo Library/Dr Jeremy Burgess; p73 Royal Botanic Gardens Kew; p75 (all) Science Photo Library/Dr Jeremy Burgess; p77 Zefa/Frank Messman; p78 (top) Allsport/Mike Powell; p78 (bottom) Frank Lane Picture Agency/A Roch; p79 Frank Lane Picture Agency/Mark Newman; p80 (both) Rex Features/NWI/The Sun; p81 (top) Rex Features/PMD; p81 (bottom) Zefa/Weir; p82 Zefa; p83 Bruce Coleman Ltd/Thomas Buchholtz; p84 Rex Features/Tim Rooke; p86 Bruce Coleman Ltd/Johnny Johnson; p87 Zefa/MM; p88 Rex Features/Tim Rooke; p89 Frank Lane Picture Agency/Fritz Polking; p91 (both) The Body Shop International plc; p92 Andrew Lambert; p93 Collections/Sandra Lousada; p 94 (both) Zefa; p95 Rex Features; p96 Zefa; p97 Kobal Collection/The Public Eye; p99 (top) Janine Wiedel; p99 (middle) Collections/Roger Scruton; p99 (inset) Zefa/Heiman; p100 (top) BD Dunn/European Space Agency; p100 (left) Topham Picturepoint/Michael Foale; p100 (bottom) Zefa/Neville Kenton; p101 (top) Walkers Crisps Ltd; p101 (bottom left) Allsport/Stu Forster; p101 (bottom middle) Allsport/Mike Hewitt; p102 (top) Robery Harding Picture Library; p102 (bottom) Andrew Lambert; p105 (top) Rex Features; p105 (bottom) Kobal Collection/Universal; p106 (top) Rex Features; p106 (middle) Robert Harding Picture Library/Vicky Skeet; p108 Hutchison Library; p109 Bruce Coleman Ltd/Geoff Doré; p110 (top) Robert Harding Picture Library/Martyn F Chillmaid; p110 (middle) Zefa; p112 Science Photo Library/David Parker; p113 (left) Rex Features/Brian Rasic; p113 (right) Rex Features; p 114 (both) Andrew Lambert; p115 Zefa; p117 (top) Frank Lane Picture Agency/B Barrell, p117 (middle) Natural History Photo Agency/NA Callow; p119 Rex Features/Gerard Davis; p120 (left) Robert Harding Picture Library/Christopher Nicholson; p120 (right) Robert Harding Picture Library/Jeremy Bright; p121 Topham Picturepoint; p123 C & S Thompson; p124 (left) Natural History Photo Agency/Brian Hawkes; p124 (right) Zefa; p125 (top) Andrew Lambert; p125 (left) Harry Smith; p125 (right) Image Bank/David de Losey; p125 (inset) Natural History Photo Agency/Stephen Dalton; p127 Still Pictures/Mark Edwards; p128 (left) Bruce Coleman Ltd/Adrian Davies; p128 (right) Rex Features/HJ; p133 (top) Allsport/Bob Martin; p133 (middle) Hutchison Library; p134 Zefa; p135 (left) Bruce Coleman Ltd/Hector Rivarola; p135 (middle) Bruce Coleman Ltd/Johnny Johnson; p135 (right) Bruce Coleman Ltd/Jules Coleman; p136 Bruce Coleman Ltd/Kim Taylor; p137 (top) Rex Features; p137 (bottom) Science Photo Library/Biophoto Associates; p138 Science Photo Library/D Phillips; p139 (both) Rex Features/NWI/The Sun; p141 (left) Frank Lane Picture Agency/Rolf Bender; p141 (right) Frank Lane Picture Agency/Silvestris; p 142 Natural History Photo Agency/Martin Wendler.

# Contents

# ■ How to use this book

This book contains some of the information and ideas scientists use in their work. It is arranged so that you learn the simpler ideas first before moving on to learn the more difficult ones. Here are some notes to help you find your way through the book.

Science Connections 1 has 10 modules. The colour code whether a module is about Biology, Chemistry or Physics.

■ **Biology**    ■ **Chemistry**    ■ **Physics**

> ◆ The text and pictures explain the science ideas.

> ◆ The bold words are important and will help you to understand the science ideas. Most of these words are explained in the glossary at the end of the book

> ◆ Each module starts with a page that shows how the science in the module is used in real-life.

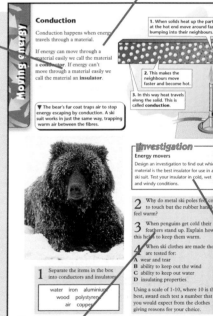

**Moving energy**

**Conduction**

Conduction happens when energy travels through a material.

If energy can move through a material easily we call the material a **conductor**. If energy can't move through a material easily we call the material an **insulator**.

▼ The bear's fur coat traps air to stop energy escaping by conduction. A ski suit works in just the same way, trapping warm air between the fibres.

**1.** When solids heat up the particles at the hot end move around faster, bumping into their neighbours.

**2.** This makes the neighbours move faster and become hot.

**3.** In this way heat travels along the solid. This is called **conduction**.

**Investigation**

**Energy movers**

Design an investigation to find out which material is the best insulator for use in a ski suit. Test your insulator in cold, wet and windy conditions.

**2** Why do metal ski poles feel cold to touch but the rubber handles feel warm?

**3** When penguins get cold their feathers stand up. Explain how this helps to keep them warm.

**4** When ski clothes are made they are tested for:
A wear and tear
B ability to keep out the wind
C ability to keep out water
D insulating properties

Using a scale of 1-10, where 10 is the best, award each test a number that you would expect from the clothes giving reasons for your choice.

**1** Separate the items in the box into conductors and insulators.

| water | iron | aluminium |
| wood | polystyrene | |
| air | copper | |

86

> ◆ Some questions do not have right or wrong answers – they ask you to discuss or present your ideas about science (as a poster, or a leaflet, or in a presentation).

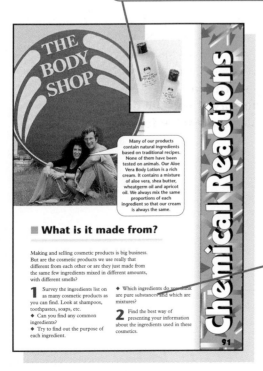

**THE BODY SHOP**

Many of our products contain natural ingredients based on traditional recipes. None of them have been tested on animals. Our Aloe Vera Body Lotion is a rich cream. It contains a mixture of aloe vera, shea butter, wheatgerm oil and apricot oil. We always mix the same proportions of each ingredient so that our cream is always the same.

**Chemical Reactions**

## ■ What is it made from?

Making and selling cosmetic products is big business. But are the cosmetic products we use really that different from each other or are they just made from the same few ingredients mixed in different amounts, with different smells?

**1** Survey the ingredients list on as many cosmetic products as you can find. Look at shampoos, toothpastes, soaps, etc.
◆ Can you find any common ingredients?
◆ Try to find out the purpose of each ingredient.

◆ Which ingredients do you think are pure substances and which are mixtures?

**2** Find the best way of presenting your information about the ingredients used in these cosmetics.

91

> ◆ The questions do not always have right or wrong answers. They ask you to think about what you already know about the subject because this is useful when you are learning about the science behind it.

◆ The key ideas section is a checklist for you to use to check that you know everything before you move on. You can also use the key ideas to revise for the end-of-module test.

◆ The questions ask about all the important ideas in the module to make sure that you understand everything before you move on.

◆ The investigation at the end of the module gives you an idea for a full investigation or research project. This means that you will need to plan, collect and analyse evidence, and make scientific conclusions. Your teacher will tell you which of these investigations or projects you need to do – there isn't time to do all of them.

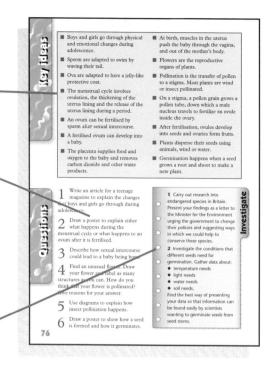

Key ideas

■ Boys and girls go through physical and emotional changes during adolescence.
■ Sperm are adapted to swim by waving their tail.
■ Ova are adapted to have a jelly-like protective coat.
■ The menstrual cycle involves ovulation, the thickening of the uterus lining and the release of the uterus lining during a period.
■ An ovum can be fertilised by sperm after sexual intercourse.
■ A fertilised ovum can develop into a baby.
■ The placenta supplies food and oxygen to the baby and removes carbon dioxide and other waste products.

■ At birth, muscles in the uterus push the baby through the vagina, and out of the mother's body.
■ Flowers are the reproductive organs of plants.
■ Pollination is the transfer of pollen to a stigma. Most plants are wind or insect pollinated.
■ On a stigma, a pollen grain grows a pollen tube, down which a male nucleus travels to fertilise an ovule inside the ovary.
■ After fertilisation, ovules develop into seeds and ovaries form fruits.
■ Plants disperse their seeds using animals, wind or water.
■ Germination happens when a seed grows a root and shoot to make a new plant.

Questions

1 Write an article for a teenage magazine to explain the changes that boys and girls go through during adolescence.
2 Draw a poster to explain either what happens during the menstrual cycle or what happens to an ovum after it is fertilised.
3 Describe how sexual intercourse could lead to a baby being born.
4 Find an unusual flower. Draw your flower and label as many structures as you can. How do you think that your flower is pollinated? Give reasons for your answer.
5 Use diagrams to explain how insect pollination happens.
6 Draw a poster to show how a seed is formed and how it germinates.

Investigate

1 Carry out research into endangered species in Britain. Present your findings as a letter to the Minister for the Environment urging the government to change their policies and suggesting ways in which we could help to conserve these species.
2 Investigate the conditions that different seeds need for germination. Gather data about:
◆ temperature needs
◆ light needs
◆ water needs
◆ soil needs.
Find the best way of presenting your data so that information can be found easily by scientists wanting to germinate seeds from seed stores.

76

◆ If you finish your work early you could complete the extra boxes. These take the science ideas you have just looked at a bit further. You may need to look things up in other books, research ideas using your library or do some more practical work.

◆ Answer the questions carefully – they are written to make sure that you understand the important ideas. If you get stuck don't give up. Read the text before the question again and check any words you don't understand in the glossary. If you still don't know the answer ask your teacher for help.

◆ The investigation boxes contain ideas for practical work. Your teacher will tell you which ones you should do. Sometimes you will need to make a plan and decide what evidence you need to collect. Your teacher must always check your plan before you do any practical work.

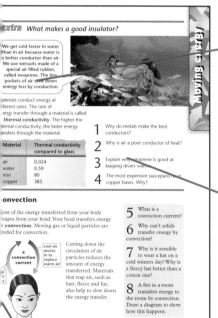

extra What makes a good insulator?

We get cold faster in water than in air because water is a better conductor than air. We use wetsuits made of a special air filled rubber, called neoprene. The tiny pockets of air slow down energy loss by conduction.

Materials conduct energy at different rates. The rate of energy transfer through a material is called thermal conductivity. The higher the thermal conductivity, the faster energy transfers through the material.

| Material | Thermal conductivity compared to glass |
| --- | --- |
| air | 0.024 |
| water | 0.59 |
| iron | 80 |
| copper | 385 |

1 Why do metals make the best conductors?
2 Why is air a poor conductor of heat?
3 Explain why neoprene is good at keeping divers warm.
4 The most expensive saucepans have copper bases. Why?

convection

Most of the energy transferred from your body escapes from the material. Your head transfers energy by convection. Moving gas or liquid particles are needed for convection.

cool air moves in to replace warm air
a convection current

Cutting down the circulation of air particles reduces the amount of energy transferred. Materials that trap air, such as hair, fleece and fur, also help to slow down the energy transfer.

5 What is a convection current?
6 Why can't solids transfer energy by convection?
7 Why is it sensible to wear a hat on a cold winters day? Why is a fleecy hat better than a cotton one?
8 A fire in a room transfers energy to the room by convection. Draw a diagram to show how this happens.

Moving energy

87

# ■ Finding your way around

There's more than one way to use a book.
Check that you are using it the best way
to get the job done.

**to do your homework**

- Check you know which pages you have to read and which questions do you need to do.

- Read slowly. Check that you understand all the words - use the **glossary** if you need to.

- The diagrams and photographs can also help you to understand the science.

**to revise for a test**

- Make sure that you are revising the right topic.

- Skim through the **key ideas** to remind yourself of the important scientific ideas in the module.

- Read through the module slowly. Check that you understand all the words – use the **glossary** if you need to. Make notes if it helps.

- Don't forget to revise the diagrams as well.

**to look something up**

- Turn to the back and use the **index** to search for the topic. Turn to the pages given in the index.

- Skim read the page until you find the topic you need.

- Read slowly. Check that you understand all the words – use the **glossary** if you need to.

# Who needs plants?

You depend on plants for all your food. This might be a surprise if you hate eating vegetables, but it is true. You eat corn and oats in breakfast cereal, wheat in bread, and vegetables or fruit with a meal. Some plants take a longer route to your digestive system. Eggs come from chickens that are fed on corn and other grains. Milk, yoghurt and cheese come from cows fed on grass. The plants at the beginning of a **food chain** provide energy for all the animals in the chain.

Plants make useful materials too, such as wood for buildings and furniture, jute and sisal for ropes and mats, and atropine to make medicines.

We also grow plants for pleasure – for making perfumes, dyes and flavours, for cut flowers and to make our gardens beautiful.

**1** Make a table like the one below listing all the products made from plants that you can think of. Two examples have been added to start you off.

| Plant | Products |
|---|---|
| pine trees | furniture, disinfectant smell, newspaper |
| flax plants | linen cloth |

**2** Why are plants at the start of food chains? Can you think of any food chain that plants do not start?

Plants

1

# How to grow a pumpkin

We need to understand how to grow plants to provide more food and useful resources.

Pumpkins are fast growing vegetables. You can eat the centres and use the shells to make containers and lanterns. A pumpkin is really a **fruit** containing seeds. They are the largest fruits we grow; the biggest weigh over 200 kg. Pumpkin plants, like all plants, need good growing conditions to make big fruit. They grow best when they are in a warm, sunny spot with plenty of water.

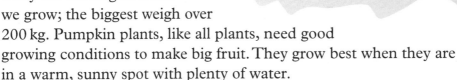

## Pumpkin Seeds

1. Plant pumpkin seeds in pots in May. Keep them inside and warm, put pots outside during the day when the young plants have two leaves.

2. Plant outside when they have four leaves and it is warmer. Dig a large hole in a sunny spot and fill with compost. Cover the compost with soil to make a mound. Cover the mound with black polythene. Microbes in the compost generate heat and release minerals for the plant. Black polythene absorbs the Sun's warmth.

3. Plant your plant in the mound of soil. Water well. Plants grow long stems along the soil surface that put out roots to take water and minerals from the soil. The stems grow 2 or 3 metres in a week when they have light, warmth, water and minerals.

4. When the fruits have grown cut off leaves that shade them to harden the skin.

1 List all the uses of a pumpkin that you can think of.

2 Why does compost in the soil help plants to grow?

3 How do the growing instructions tell you to provide extra warmth for the pumpkin plant?

4 List four things that pumpkin plants need to grow well. Do all plants need the same things to grow well?

## investigation

**Grow it!**

Design an experiment to investigate the effect of temperature on **germinating** cress seeds. How can you make sure that your test is fair?

Ask your teacher to check your plan before you start.

# ■ Plants for eating

## Shoots
Shoots are the fastest growing parts of a plant. They produce new stems, leaves, **flowers**, **fruit** and **seeds**. There is a main shoot on the tip of the stem and side shoots from buds on the stem. We eat fruit and seeds, such as apples, tomatoes and nuts.

## Leaves
Leaves make food during **photosynthesis**. Leaves are like factories, with a supply of raw materials which they make into products. They keep some of what they make for their own needs and export the rest to other parts of the plant. Plants need sunlight to make food. Sunlight is trapped best by large, flat leaves with a big surface area. We eat plant leaves, such as spinach, cabbage and herbs.

flower

leaf stalk

leaf

tendril

vein

mid rib

seed pod

stem

bud

root

## Stems
The stem holds the leaves up in the air. The stem always grows towards sunlight. Stems transport the products made by leaves to other parts of the plant. They also bring water and **minerals** from the soil to the leaves. We eat plant stems, such as celery and rhubarb.

## Buds
Where a leaf stalk joins a stem a tiny **bud** develops. This can grow out into a side shoot. We eat plant buds, such as brussels sprouts.

## Roots
Roots absorb water and minerals from the soil and anchor plants in the soil. In some plants, roots act as a food store. We eat plant roots, such as carrots and potatoes.

5 What is the function of a leaf?

6 List two jobs done by stems.

7 How can a plant continue to grow if the tip is eaten by a grazing animal?

8 Make lists of the things that you eat that are: fruit, leaves, roots and seeds.

## Trapping sunlight

A plant's leaves are arranged to catch as much light as possible. If you look down on a plant from above you can see that the leaves spread out to make a pattern. Nearby leaves hardly overlap each other so that they do not block each others' sunlight. The pattern the leaves make is called a **leaf mosaic**.

▲ A leaf mosaic.

**9** Look at the leaf mosaic picture carefully. How many squares are covered by leaf? How many squares are there in the grid altogether? What proportion of the grid area is covered by leaf? What percentage of light does the plant not catch within the grid?

**10** Why do you think that it is so important for plants to grow their leaves in mosaic patterns?

### *investigation*

**Mosaics**

Put a potted plant on a sheet of graph paper with a bright light overhead. Draw round the shadows of the plant's leaves. Count squares to calculate the area covered by the leaves. Draw a large square or circle round the edges of the leaves. What proportion of the area is covered by leaves?

### *extra* *Find the light*

Plants always grow towards light because they need to find light in order to make food by **photosynthesis**.

**1** How could you investigate how light intensity or the direction of light affects the growth of radish seedlings? How could you make your test fair? Discuss your plan with your teacher and if you have time carry out your investigation.

**2** Find out how **gravity** can affect the way that plants grow. Produce a poster to show your findings.

# What are cells?

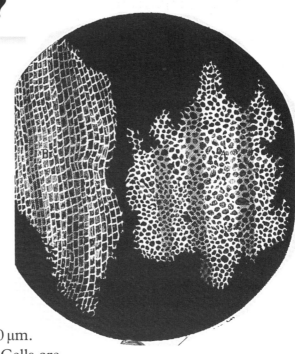

▶ These pictures of the structure of cork were drawn by a scientist in the 17th Century called Robert Hooke. Hooke made one of the earliest microscopes and began to look in detail at how plants were constructed. He saw that plants were made from thousands of small 'compartments', which he called **cells**. As better microscopes were produced, scientists discovered that all organisms were made of cells.

Cells are very small, between 0.5 and 20 µm. 1 µm is one thousandth of a millimetre. Cells are too small and **transparent** to see without the help of a microscope and a stain to make their features stand out.

The smallest a human eye can see is about 0.1 mm so you can't see cells with just your eyes. Light microscopes can be used to see objects of about 0.2 µm so we can use them to see actual cells.

## Plant cells

Plant cells seen with a microscope have regular shapes with distinct boundaries.

cell membrane

the **cell wall** is made of tough **cellulose** fibres to support and strengthen the cell.

**chloroplasts** in cells from the green parts of plants make food by photosynthesis.

cytoplasm

the **nucleus** controls the cell's activity.

the **vacuole** contains fluids and dissolved nutrients. The size changes according to the amount of water the plant has.

If you could find a typical plant cell it would look like this picture, but most cells are **specialised** to do a particular job. Supporting cells have thicker, stronger walls. Root cells do not have chloroplasts, but may have starch stores instead.

1 Explain what each of the following structures do: cell wall, chloroplast, nucleus, vacuole.

2 Draw and label a typical animal cell. List three differences between your animal cell and the plant cell opposite.

5

## investigation

### What's in a cell?

Examine cells from samples of potato, onion and moss. Draw three cells from each sample. Label them.

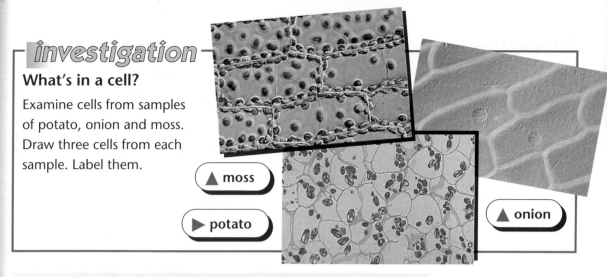

▲ moss

▶ potato

▲ onion

3  In what ways did your onion and potato cells look different from the plant cell on page 5?

# ■ What happens in a leaf?

Plants can make everything that they need from simple chemicals in the air and soil. The most important substance they make is a sugar, called **glucose**, by **photosynthesis**. Plant cells use glucose as:

◆ an energy source for their activities
◆ a raw material for making other substances.

Most glucose is made in specialised leaf cells. Chloroplasts inside the cells contain green **chlorophyll** which traps sunlight to drive chemical reactions.

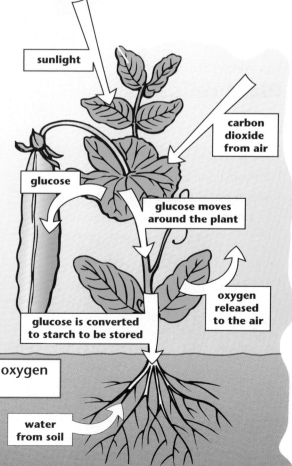

sunlight

carbon dioxide from air

glucose

glucose moves around the plant

oxygen released to the air

glucose is converted to starch to be stored

water from soil

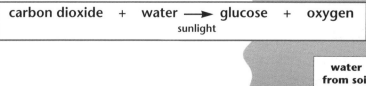

carbon dioxide  +  water  ⟶  glucose  +  oxygen
                        sunlight

# Supplying the cells

## Energy

Sunlight energy drives photosynthesis so plants need to trap as much sunlight as possible.

◆ The flat surface of the leaf is held at right angles to the Sun.

◆ The stem grows so that it holds leaves clear of nearby plants' leaves.

◆ The leaves are arranged so that they do not shade each other.

## Gases

Carbon dioxide enters leaves through small holes, called **stomata**, scattered over the surface of leaves. Oxygen, released in photosynthesis, escapes from the leaf through the stomata. Stomata close at night when there isn't enough light for photosynthesis. A pair of **guard cells** on either side of the hole change shape to open and close it.

## Water

Water is absorbed from soil and carried through the plant by transporting cells called **xylem vessels**. Xylem vessels run up the stem, through leaf stalks into leaves. There they run through the midrib and branch out into the veins, supplying every part of a leaf.

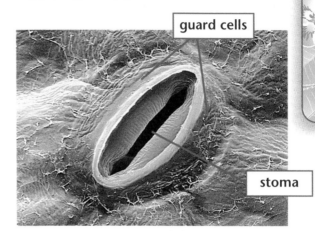

guard cells

stoma

## investigation

### Looking for stomata

Make an impression of the top and bottom of a leaf using nail varnish. Use a microscope to look at the stomata.

Are there more stomata on the top or the bottom? Try to estimate how big they are. Try to estimate how many there are in a mm².

4 Make a list of materials plants take in from their surroundings.

5 Why do plants need minerals?

6 What is the green substance in leaves called? What is its job?

7 Explain why the mouse could survive in Bell Jar B?

Priestley put a mouse in a bell-jar in which a candle had burnt until it went out.

The mouse could not live.

Priestley put a plant into a bell-jar in which he had burnt a candle.

After a while the air could keep a mouse alive.

## extra  *Chlorophyll colour*

Extract the green colour from a leaf. Use chromatography to find out if there is just one coloured substance in a leaf or if there are more.

# ■ Journey into a green interior

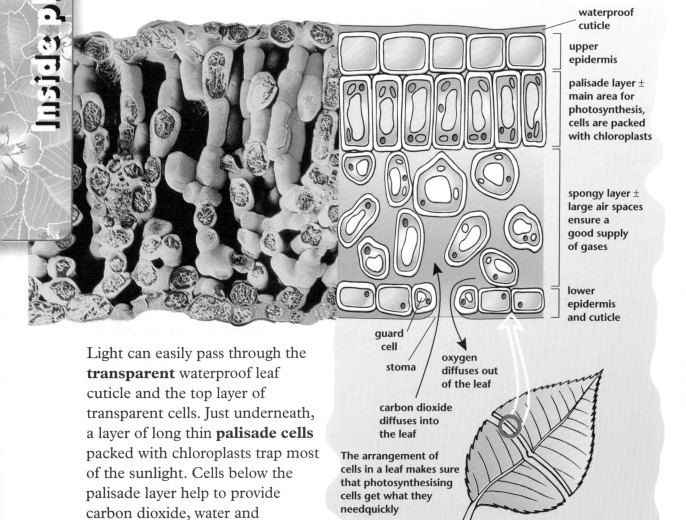

waterproof cuticle

upper epidermis

palisade layer ± main area for photosynthesis, cells are packed with chloroplasts

spongy layer ± large air spaces ensure a good supply of gases

lower epidermis and cuticle

guard cell

stoma

oxygen diffuses out of the leaf

carbon dioxide diffuses into the leaf

The arrangement of cells in a leaf makes sure that photosynthesising cells get what they need quickly

Light can easily pass through the **transparent** waterproof leaf cuticle and the top layer of transparent cells. Just underneath, a layer of long thin **palisade cells** packed with chloroplasts trap most of the sunlight. Cells below the palisade layer help to provide carbon dioxide, water and minerals. They can also photosynthesise using any light which escapes through the palisade layer.

8 How does the shape of a leaf help it to photosynthesise efficiently?

9 How do the structures in the leaf help to hold it in the light?

10 What are the two substances made in photosynthesis?

# Using glucose

Some of the glucose is used as soon as it is made for the cell's energy needs. Some glucose is used to make cellulose for cell walls, fats and proteins. Plants also need minerals from the soil to make these. Any left over glucose is made into starch. This is kept in the cell until it can be moved to stores in roots, seeds and fruits.

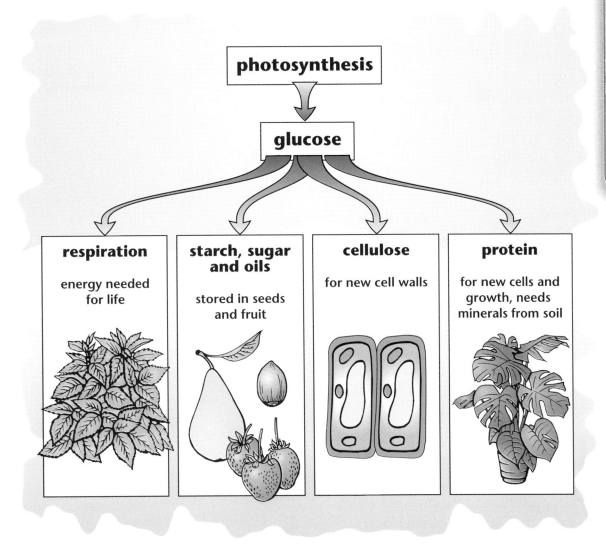

Plants make glucose when there is enough light. Glucose is made into **starch** in the leaf cells temporarily. Later, starch is changed back into glucose so that it can be moved to parts of the plant which need it. Any plant that has been photosynthesising will have starch in its leaves.

---

## investigation

### Detecting starch in leaves

Test small sections of leaf to find out if they contain starch.

What can you tell from whether the leaf contains starch or not?

---

11 Write down the job of each of the following: palisade cell, stomata, chlorophyll, xylem.

12 In a photosynthesis investigation why would you use the following: iodine solution, hot ethanol?

13 Gardeners keep some plants in greenhouses in the winter. Heating the greenhouse with a paraffin heater helps the plants to grow. Explain two different ways in which a paraffin heater can help plants to grow.

## extra Light and photosynthesis

Jane and Michael wanted to know whether all of a plant needs to be in light to make starch. They put a geranium plant in a dark place for two days to use up any starch stores in its leaves.

Jane and Michael each took a square of black paper and cut the shape of their initial in the centre. They put the black paper squares on the top of two large healthy leaves on the geranium plant. They placed another plain black paper square underneath each leaf and fastened the two together with sticky tape.

The plant was left near a lamp for a day. The two leaves that had been covered were picked and tested for starch.

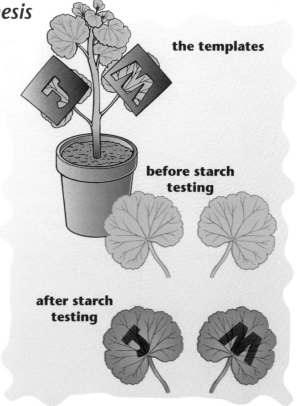
the templates

before starch testing

after starch testing

1 Why was the plant put in a dark place for 2 days before the investigation?

2 How did this help to make it a fair test?

3 Why did the leaves have black paper underneath as well as on top?

4 Describe how would you test a leaf for starch.

5 Explain why the leaves had black shapes in the centre but were brownish yellow round the edge.

## investigation

**Patchy food**

Variegated plants have yellow, white or pink patches on the leaves. Chlorophyll has not developed in these patches. How could you find out whether these patches can photosynthesise? Would you expect to find starch all over the leaf?

# At the root of the problem

◀ People sometimes find nasty cracks in their house walls after a hot, dry summer. The soil shrinks when water evaporates from the soil, then swells again when it rains in the winter. The soil movement weakens the foundations and stresses the walls so that they crack.

Trees near a house cause exactly the same problem because tree roots take in a huge amount of water from soil during a hot sunny day. Trees have a large network of roots to absorb the water they need. Roots even grow into drains in search of water. This causes lots of problems. Insurance companies keep records of claims due to damage by tree roots.

| Tree | Half the incidents of damage occurred within (m) | Furthest distance to damage (m) | % drain blockage caused |
|------|--------------------------------------------------|----------------------------------|-------------------------|
| apple/pear | 4 | 10 | 2.0 |
| birch | 4 | 10 | 5.5 |
| conifer | 2.5 | 10 | 2.5 |
| oak | 9.5 | 30 | 3.5 |
| poplar | 11 | 30 | 24 |
| willow | 7 | 30 | 18.5 |

1 Use the information in the table to draw a bar chart to be used in a garden centre to show customers how far tree roots can spread and how much damage each type of tree can do.

2 Which tree type seems most likely to cause problems if your house is built nearby?

3 If someone had a small garden but wanted a tree in it what would you recommend? Why have you chosen this type?

4 How far can an oak tree's roots extend round the tree?

# Roots

A plant's roots:

◆ anchor it firmly against the wind
◆ stabilise it and help keep it upright
◆ absorb water from the soil
◆ absorb minerals from the soil.

Roots grow between soil particles. Soil particles are surrounded by a thin layer of water which plant roots can absorb. The water layer also carries dissolved minerals from the soil.

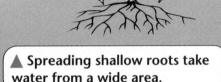

◀ Tap roots grow deep into the soil and anchor the plant against the wind and grazing animals. Deep roots take water from far below the surface.

▲ Spreading shallow roots take water from a wide area.

◀ These plants grow on other plants for support. Their roots take moisture from the humid air around plants in a rain forest.

## Looking at roots

The outer layers of a root are tough and waterproof, protecting it from sharp soil particles and gnawing soil inhabitants. Just like shoots, roots grow from their tips. New cells produced just behind the tip expand and force the root tip further between the soil particles.

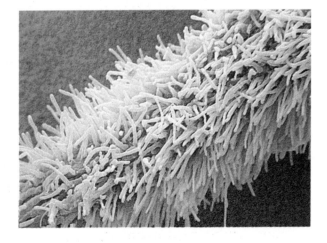

▲ Water is absorbed through special cells shaped like fine threads, called **root hairs**. Root hairs grow just behind the growing tip of the root. As a root pushes further into the soil new root hairs form and the older ones break off.

### *investigation*

#### Looking at roots

Gently lift out some of the plants taking care not to damage the roots. Tease out some of the roots and use a microscope to see the fine extensions which absorb water.

# Taking in water?

Stephen Hales lived near Kew in London nearly 300 years ago. He was interested in how plants worked. In one of his investigations he tried to measure the movement of water taken in by a plant. He cut down a vine he had so that about 17 cm of stem was left above ground. He fastened glass tubing to the stump. The sections of tube he used reached to about 7 m high. Nothing came out of the stem into the tubing at first, so he poured some water into the tube above the stem.

> ▶ These pictures are from Stephen Hales' book, *Vegetable Statiks*. They show some of the experiments he tried on plants in his garden.

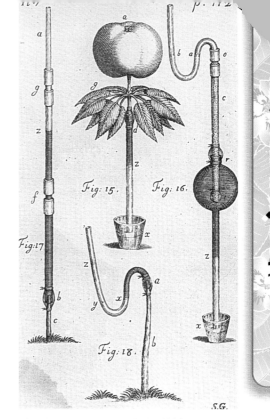

Most of this water was absorbed by the vine stump during the day, but the next morning there was water 7 cm deep above the stump. During that day the water level rose by another 20 cm, the following night by another 8 cm, then more the next day. Eventually the column of water was over 6 m high before leaking joints brought the investigation to a halt.

**5** List two things that roots absorb from the soil.

**6** How can you explain the appearance of water in the tube in Stephen Hales' experiment?

**7** Why do gardeners try to keep a clump of soil round the roots of a plant when they move it from one part of the garden to another?

---

- Plants are the start of food chains. They provide energy for other organisms in a chain.

- Plants grow best when they are kept in warm, moist conditions with plenty of light and the minerals they need.

- All organisms are made from cells.

- Plant cells have a cell wall and a vacuole. They can also have chloroplasts.

- Plants make glucose during photosynthesis, from carbon dioxide and water. They release oxygen as a waste product.

- Plants use chlorophyll to trap energy from the Sun.

- The structure of a plant allows it to photosynthesise efficiently.

- Glucose from photosynthesis is converted to other substances including starch for storage.

- Plants take in water and minerals from the soil through root hairs.

Moving water

Key ideas

**1** List the four things that plants need to grow best.

**2** What is meant by a 'leaf mosaic'?

**3** Greenhouses are often lit by fluorescent lights during the winter. How does lighting the greenhouse help the plants to grow and develop?

**4** What are the functions of palisade cells and root hair cells? How are they specialised to cary out their functions?

**5** Describe three ways in which glucose is used by plants.

**6** What are stomata – what do they do and how do they work?

**7** Why is it important for stomata to close at night when the plant is not photosynthesising?

**8** Copy and complete these notes. Use the words in the box to help you.

| warmth | light | food | green | Sun |
|--------|-------|------|-------|-----|
| | water | photosynthesis | | |

Agriculture is an industry that relies on sunlight. The process by which _____ plants use the energy of the _____ to turn carbon dioxide from the air and _____ into glucose is called _____.

Photosynthesis allows plants to grow and provides _____ for animals. Plants can grow quickly when conditions are favourable. They need _____, water, and plenty of _____ to grow well.

**9** Water plants release oxygen into the water. Why are water plants so important for the survival of water animals?

How could you investigate whether or not a market gardener needs to ensure a good supply of carbon dioxide to the plants in their greenhouse?

You may find it useful to know that a small beaker of potassium hydroxide solution absorbs carbon dioxide from the air around it.

**Safety: potassium hydroxide solution is corrosive and poisonous**

▲ One day our **Sun** will explode. When this happens, the **planets**, including the Earth and all the life on it, will be destroyed. If we are to survive, we will need to find other places outside our **Solar System** to live. But, don't be too alarmed, there is plenty of time for us to work out how to do it and survive!

# ■ Our destiny in space

We have already managed to send spacecraft to explore our family of planets. We have sent humans into space for over a year and brought them back safely. However, astronauts have never travelled further than our Moon, and they have not yet grown their own food in space.

Although the explosion of the Sun will not affect the Earth in your lifetime, there are other events in space which do affect you.

**1** Think of reasons why it is difficult for astronauts to grow food in space?

**2** Astronauts staying in space for a long time become bad tempered and annoyed with their fellow travellers. Can you explain why being in space affects them in this way?

**3** To go on really long space journeys, it is thought that astronauts will need to be put into suspended animation, so that they do not age on the long journey. What problems might this present when they need to travel back to Earth too?

**4** How does what happens in space affect your life?

# History of the stars

From the earliest records of history we can see that humans have always been interested in how the stars, Sun and Moon move about us and how they affect our lives.

The ancient Egyptians and Chinese believed that the Earth was flat and floated on a never-ending sea. They believed that the Earth was covered by a dome where their gods lived and moved. Surprising events, such as **comets**, were thought to be signals from the Gods.

**Start of the Greek Empire**

One of the earliest astronomers was Thales, who lived in the 6th century BC. He believed that the flat Earth was at the centre of the Universe and that the planets, Sun and Moon all travelled round it in circles.

In 300 BC Aristarchus of Samos calculated the size of Earth and suggested that the planets went around the Sun.

During the medieval age people still believed that the Earth was at the centre of the universe. The powerful Catholic Church agreed with this because they believed that God had made Earth the centre of everything.

In 1543 a polish monk, Nicolas Copernicus, wrote a book suggesting that the Earth, Moon and other planets moved around the Sun in circles. The Church in Europe did not agree – they said that his work was disrespectful to God. Scientists who agreed with Copernicus were often imprisoned or executed by the Church.

1 Imagine that you lived at some time before the 16th Century. Write a letter to a friend describing what you believed the Earth and Solar System were like.

2 Why do you think that the Church in Europe was so against the ideas put forward by Copernicus?

In 350 BC Aristotle proved that the Earth was a sphere.

## 146 BC End of the Greek Empire, start of the Roman Empire

Ptolemy was an astronomer in the 2nd century BC. It was his model of the universe, with its 'celestial spheres', that was used until the 16th Century. Understanding in science does not always move in the way that you might expect!

## AD 395 the end of the Roman Empire

## The Dark Ages

# A family of planets

Today we accept that the Earth is just one of the nine planets that **orbit** the Sun, to make our Solar System. The planets do not give out light of their own, they **reflect** light given out by the Sun.

► The Sun is made of dense hydrogen gas and releases light during nuclear reactions.

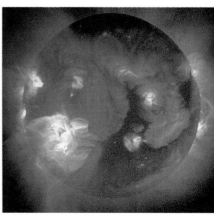

We have sent robot probes to map the surfaces, test the atmospheres and even sample the rocks on many planets.

We also know how special Earth is. No other planet has life on it. It is the only planet with the right climate and temperature. If we damage Earth, there is no other planet in our Solar System that we can move to!

Finally, in 1609, Johannes Keppler used observations and mathematics to prove that the Church was wrong and that the planets moved around the Sun in ellipses, not circles.

# The Solar System

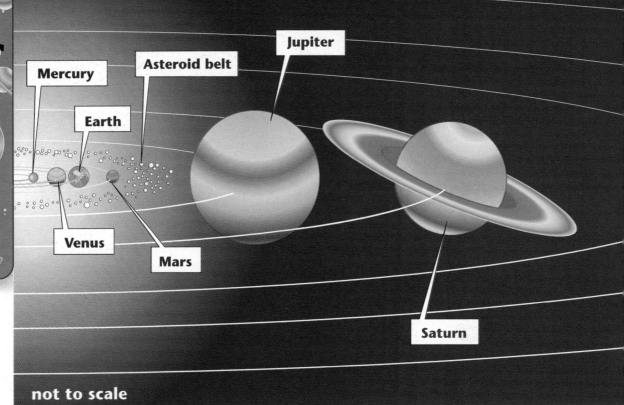

Mercury

Asteroid belt

Jupiter

Earth

Venus

Mars

Saturn

not to scale

| Planet | Distance from Sun compared to Earth | Length of year in Earth years | Diameter compared to Earth | Temperature in °C |
|---|---|---|---|---|
| Mercury | 0.38 | 0.24 | 0.38 | 350 |
| Venus | 0.72 | 0.62 | 0.95 | 460 |
| Earth | 1 | 1 | 1 | 15 |
| Mars | 1.5 | 1.9 | 0.52 | 20 |
| (Asteroid belt) | 2 to 4 | 3 to 8 | | |
| Jupiter | 5.2 | 11.9 | 11.1 | -23 |
| Saturn | 9.52 | 29.5 | 9.5 | 120 |
| Uranus | 19.2 | 84.0 | 3.7 | -180 |
| Neptune | 30.1 | 164.8 | 3.49 | -220 |
| Pluto | 39.4 | 248 | 0.5 | -230 |
| (Proxima Centauri) | 266 000 | | | |

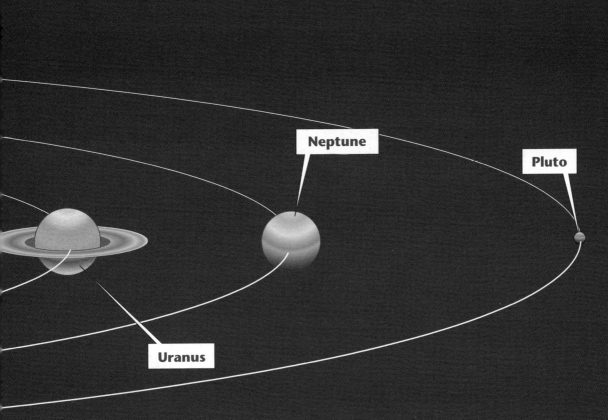

| Features | Number of Satellites |
|---|---|
| Moon-like craters on surface | 0 |
| dense, acidic atmosphere, high temperatures caused by the greenhouse effect | 0 |
| only planet with liquid water and life | 1 |
| red planet with polar ice caps like Earth | 2 |
| many rocks and minor planets | |
| made of gases and liquids, large red spot on the surface | 16 |
| has visible rings around it | 16 |
| discovered in 1781, atmosphere of hydrogen and methane | 5 |
| discovered in 1846, atmosphere of hydrogen | 2 |
| discovered in 1930, very elliptical orbit | 1 |
| our closest star, after the Sun | |

## investigation

### Model planets

Make a scale model of the planets. You could use an object the size of a basketball to represent Jupiter.

Work out how far from the Sun you would need to put Proxima Centauri in your model.

**3** In ancient times the number 7 had a special significance as a 'perfect' number. What were the 7 astronomical objects known to exist 2000 years ago?

**4** The order of the planets can be remembered using this sentence:
**My Very Energetic Maiden Aunt Just Swam Under North Pier**
**a** What is the order of the planets from the Sun?
**b** Make up your own sentence to help you to remember the order of the planets.

**5** List the planets in order of size starting with the largest.

## investigation

### Planet patterns

Put the data about the planets into a spreadsheet which can produce graphs. Use the graphs you produce to look for some patterns or trends in the data and describe any that you see. If you don't have a spreadsheet to use, draw your graphs using the data in the table.

## extra *Things that go bump...*

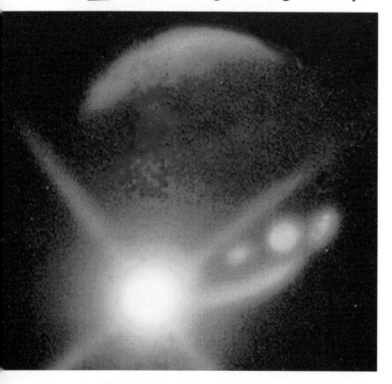

▲ The comet known as Shoemaker-Levy crashed into Jupiter in 1994. According to Japanese astronomer Isshi Tabe, there is evidence that Jupiter is hit every 300 years or so by a major comet.

Further out from Neptune and Pluto are lumps of ice and rock. If one of these lumps changes its orbit, it could be pulled towards the Sun. When it gets near the Sun, it becomes hotter, moves faster and releases water vapour and dust which form a tail. The ball of ice and rock has now become a **comet**. Some comets orbit the Sun for hundreds of years, others are quickly burnt up. Sometimes comets even hit planets.

**1** How are comets and planets different?

**2** Bright comets, with large tails often only appear once or twice. Dim ones may appear in the sky many times. Explain why.

# ■ Earth spinning

It may not feel like it, but the Earth is moving very quickly. Because the movement is a steady one, you don't normally notice it. The Earth is spinning and carrying you and everything else on the Earth with it.

## Day or night?

daytime

light from Sun

night-time

▲ The spinning of the Earth causes our night and day. When the side of the Earth that you are on points towards the Sun, it is daytime. As the Earth spins, you are carried round away from the Sun into the Earth's shadow and this is night-time.

◀▶ As the Earth spins, the Sun seems to move across the sky during the day, and the stars seem to move round us at night. A day is the time it takes for the Sun and the stars to appear in the same position again.

**1** The Greeks thought that the Earth was at the centre of the universe and that the Sun and planets orbited the Earth. What evidence is there to support these ideas?

**2** What evidence could you use to prove to a Greek astronomer that it is the Earth that orbits the Sun, not the Sun that orbits the Earth?

**3** Draw a poster to explain why day and night are at different times in Britain and America.

## investigation

### Time trial

Push a stick into the ground through a piece of paper. Every hour mark where the shadow of the stick is on the paper. Why does the shadow move?

On another day, use the stick and paper as a sundial to tell the time. How accurate is your sundial

## Satellites

The six satellites that we use to watch the weather orbit the Earth around the equator. They move at the same speed as the Earth turns, so they stay over the same bit of the Earth all the time. We collect information from these satellites every 30 minutes so that we can follow changes in the weather as they happen. Using this information we can forecast what the weather is likely to do over the next few days.

Other satellites are used to collect information about everything from what crops are growing, to where troops are moving. Data from these satellites is also used by businesses, such as oil companies looking for good places to explore.

These satellites travel right round the Earth, over the North and South poles. The satellites keep travelling in the same way all the time, but because the Earth is spinning, the satellite scans a different part each time it makes an **orbit**. This means that only a few satellites need to orbit the Earth, to examine all of it.

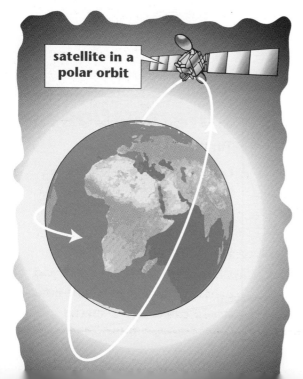

satellite in a polar orbit

▲ A satellite image of Europe.

## investigation
### Satellite spotting

On a clear night look into the sky and try to spot a satellite. It will look rather like a star, but will move from South to North or North to South, taking several minutes to cross the sky.

Look again about 90 minutes later, and you could see it in the sky again, but this time much further to the West.

4 Aeroplanes and ground surveys used to be the main ways of gathering data about the Earth's surface.
**a** Suggest reasons why satellites are better than planes and ground surveys for gathering information.
**b** What are the difficulties of using satellites that the other methods do not have?

5 It is expensive to build and to launch a satellite. Why are businesses willing to spend so much money?

## extra  *When is a day not a day?*

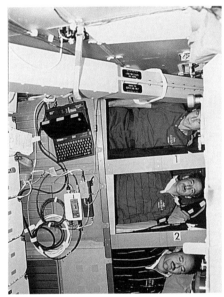

◀ Humans who travel in space cannot rely on Earth days and nights to organise their lives. So, would astronauts who travel in space for years at a time be able to keep to 24-hour Earth days?

Like most animals, our 'body clocks' are linked to a 24-hour day. We go to sleep at about the same time every day, and wake up at about the same time.

To find out about the effect of space travel on the human body clock, scientists kept people in dimly lit places. The people woke when they thought it was morning and went to sleep when they thought it was night-time. After a week some people thought a day was 33 hours long! Everyone had their own body clock which was different from everyone else's. Your body clock is controlled by a small part of your brain, and you cannot change it.

1 On most days, you have to get up in time to get to school. But, you may be able to choose when to get up and go to bed during the holidays. Carry out a survey of your friends to find out when they go to bed during their holidays. See if there is a pattern in the behaviour. Suggest reasons for any pattern you find.

2 Astronauts in orbit around the Earth can have many 'days' compared to one of ours. Explain why.

3 Imagine you went into space on a long journey, and judged time just on your internal clock. People on Earth expect you to return on a certain day, or even year! If your internal clock makes your days longer than 24 hours, will you return on a date that is later or earlier than you thought? Explain your answer.

# ■ Moon movement

In 1609, Galileo Galilei built a simple telescope to look at the **Moon**. He was the first person to really look at the surface of the Moon in detail and realised that we only ever see one side of it. It was only after space rockets had been invented and sent round the Moon, that we were able to get pictures of the far side.

The Moon does not give out light of its own. We can see the Moon because it **reflects** light from the Sun.

The Moon spins and orbits the Earth. The Moon takes about 28 days to travel round the Earth, but it also takes 28 days to spin round once, this is why the same side of the Moon always faces the Earth.

## Moon phases

As the Moon moves round the Earth, we get changing views of it depending on how much of it is lit by the Sun. These changes are called the **phases** of the Moon. Many organisms, such as midges and giant turtles, have breeding cycles which seem to be linked to the phases of the Moon.

▼ The Moon's phases.

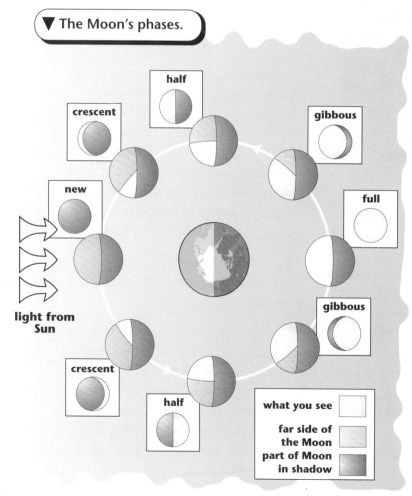

half

crescent

gibbous

new

full

light from Sun

gibbous

crescent

half

| what you see | |
| far side of the Moon | |
| part of Moon in shadow | |

6 Some people call the far side of the Moon, 'the dark side'. Is the far side of the Moon always in the dark? Explain your answer.

7 The start of many religious festivals is linked to the New Moon. Find out about one of them and draw a poster to show your findings.

**Changing Moons**

Draw what the Moon looks like each night for a month. Label your diagrams.

When was there a full Moon? Predict when the next full Moon will be.

## Tides

The side of the Earth that is closest to the Moon feels a strong pull towards the Moon due to **gravity**. This pulls water towards to Moon, and causes the seas to be deeper on that side of the Earth by about 30 cm. Because the Earth is spinning, different places on Earth experience this deeper water at different times. This deeper water causes our **tides**.

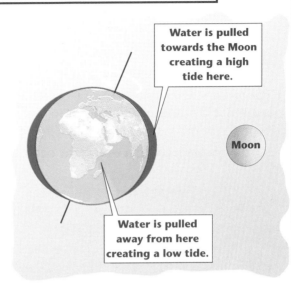

Water is pulled towards the Moon creating a high tide here.

Moon

Water is pulled away from here creating a low tide.

▲ A solar eclipse.

## Eclipses

A few times a year the Moon moves directly between the Sun and Earth, so that a shadow is cast onto the Earth. If you are standing where the shadow falls on the Earth, the Sun disappears and it goes very dark, even though it is daytime. The event does not last for very long, because the Moon moves out of the way fairly quickly. This is a **solar eclipse**.

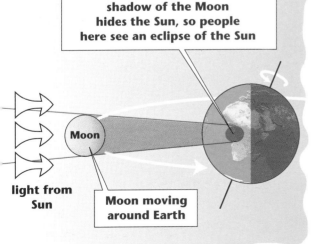

shadow of the Moon hides the Sun, so people here see an eclipse of the Sun

Moon

light from Sun

Moon moving around Earth

8 A **lunar eclipse** is an eclipse of the Moon. Draw a diagram to show what you think happens during a lunar eclipse. Explain your diagram and then find out from your teacher if you are right.

# ■ Earth in orbit

The shape of the Earth's orbit around the Sun is an **ellipse**, this is a flattened circle. This means that the distance between the Earth and the Sun changes slightly each day.

The Earth completes one orbit of the Sun every 365.26 days. We can work out this time accurately because it takes this time before the Sun and the stars are in exactly the same place again. To make life easier, most of our years are 365 days long with a leap year of 366 days every fourth year to use up the extra quarter of a day from each year.

**9** A friend says that they only have a real birthday once every four years. What is the date of their birthday? Why does this date only occur every fourth year?

**10** One person says that 'a year is 365 days'. Are they right or wrong. Explain your answer.

## Seasons

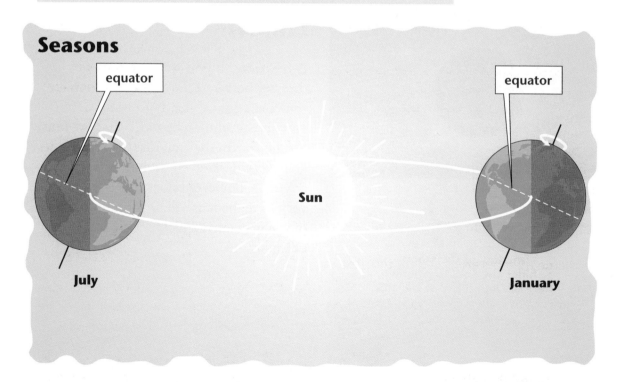

equator

equator

Sun

July

January

The Earth's spin is tilted. This means that sometimes the northern hemisphere of the Earth is pointing slightly towards the Sun and the southern hemisphere is pointing slightly away from it. When this happens, the northern hemisphere experiences summer and the southern hemisphere experiences winter. Six months later the situation is reversed: the northern hemisphere has winter, and the southern hemisphere has summer.

# extra  *Catch a falling star?*

▲ A meteor trail.

If a rock from space enters our atmosphere it burns up and we see it as a fast moving point of light. These rocks are called **meteors** or shooting stars.

When the Earth passes through the rubbish left behind by a comet the number of meteors entering our atmosphere is very high.

Very large meteors are called **meteorites**. They do not burn up completely but reach the ground sometimes making large holes. About six meteorites hit the Earth each year.

It is estimated that about 100 000 000 kg of meteors hit the Earth's atmosphere each year! If that was in one lump it would be a lump of rock about the size of a football stadium. Luckily most meteorites are smaller than 1 mm in diameter.

1 A friend of yours is very worried that with so much material hitting the Earth every year, they might get hit themselves. Explain why they are unlikely to be hit by a meteorite.

2 The best meteor showers are:

Quadratids      January 1st to 6th
Aquarids        July 15th to August 15th
Persieds        July 25th to August 18th
Orionids        October 16th to 26th
Geminids        December 7th to 15th

**a** When is the best time to look for meteors?
**b** Explain why the timing of meteor showers is not completely random.

3 Try making craters like the ones meteorites have made on the Moon. What will you use as the meteorites? What sort of surfaces might work well? You could try fine sand, flour or even moist plaster of Paris. How can you make sure that your investigation is fair?

# ■ Discovering gravity

▶ Our understanding of how the Solar System works, took a huge leap forward in 1666. Isaac Newton was trying to work out why the Moon orbits the Earth. While sitting in his garden, Newton observed an apple falling from a tree and wondered why the apple fell, rather than moving sideways or upwards. At that moment he made the connection between why objects fall, why we feel **weight**, and why the Moon stays in orbit. The link is the attraction force **gravity**.

Newton argued that all objects have **mass** and that all objects have an attraction force between them. This attraction force is gravity. The larger the objects are, and the closer they are to each other, the greater the force of attraction.

All objects on Earth have weight because of the gravitational attraction between the object and the Earth. When an object is dropped, gravitational force makes it fall faster and faster to the ground.

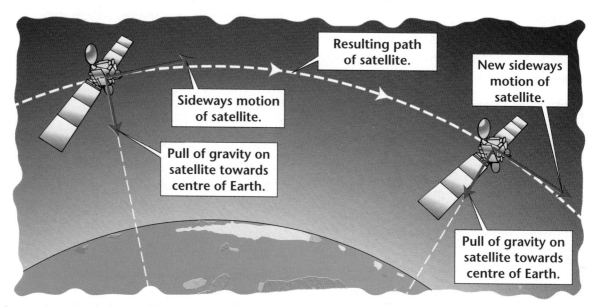

Resulting path of satellite.

New sideways motion of satellite.

Sideways motion of satellite.

Pull of gravity on satellite towards centre of Earth.

Pull of gravity on satellite towards centre of Earth.

Gravity also keeps the Earth and other planets orbiting the Sun. Although the Sun is 150 000 000 km away from the Earth, it has so much matter in it, that it produces a very strong force of gravity, and this stops the Earth escaping. Without gravity, the Earth would move at a high speed in a straight line away from the Sun, and we would all die!

1 Find out more about the work of Newton. Do you think that he was a truly great scientist? Why?

2 In your own words, explain why the Moon stays in orbit around the Earth.

## *extra* *What is weightlessness?*

In spacecraft which orbit the Earth, astronauts appear to be **weightless**. Objects and people float about inside the spacecraft. However, the objects have not escaped from gravity and become weightless. They are falling at the same rate as all the other objects in the spacecraft and so appear to be weightless.

> ▶ It may not look like it, but the astronauts in the Space Shuttle are falling. The Shuttle is falling too, so they appear to float inside it.

Scientists have found that some experiments can be carried out more successfully in conditions of weightlessness, sometimes called **microgravity**.

1 Find out about an experiment that is being carried out in space or under microgravity. Give a presentation about what the experiment is being used to study to the rest of your class.

2 What effects do you think that weightlessness would have on an astronaut's body if they were in space for long periods?

3 What other factors have to be taken into account when we are planning on sending astronauts into space for long periods?

**Key ideas**

- Our ideas about the Solar System have changed during our history.

- We know there are other planets because they reflect sunlight.

- Over several months the planets move across the night sky.

- Robots can be used to learn about other planets and comets.

- Satellites are used to collect information about the Earth.

- The Earth spins once a day. The side of the Earth which is facing the Sun is in daytime. The side of the Earth facing away from the Sun is in night-time.

- The Moon orbits the Earth in about 28 days.

- The phases of the Moon occur because it orbits the Earth.

- The Earth orbits the Sun once a year (about 365 days).

- Our seasons happen because the Earth's axis is tilted.

- The Earth's gravity attracts objects towards it, and causes objects to have weight.

- The Earth's gravity holds the Moon close to the Earth.

- The Sun's gravity holds planets and comets in the Solar System.

**1**
**a** List these items in order of size:

| meteorite | star | planet | comet | Solar System |

**b** Name one item from the list that is seen because it reflects sunlight.

**c** Name one item from the list which emits light.

**2** Which is the closest star to Earth?

**3** Imagine you are trying to convince someone of the ideas listed below. Image that satellites, planes and cars have not been invented yet. What arguments would you use, or what demonstrations would you carry out?

**a** The Earth is a sphere and not flat.

**b** The Earth is spinning, not stationary.

**d** The stars are very far away, much further than the Sun.

**e** Comets are outside our atmosphere, and not inside.

**4** Spacecraft can be hit by meteors and rubbish from old satellites and spacecraft.

**a** Suggest problems that could result from a spacecraft being hit.

**b** Suggest ways of protecting spacecraft from meteors and space rubbish.

**5** A friend says that "there is no point in learning anything about astronomy, because nothing in space affect our lives". Write an answer to this comment.

**6** Find out as much as you can about how the Moon's phases affect the lives of organisms. Give a presentation about your findings to the rest of your class.

**7** Draw a time line for the development of our understanding about the Solar System. Use the information in this module and research in other books to add as much information as you can. Present your time line as a poster.

Write a travel brochure for space holidaymakers travelling around the Solar System in the next century.

Include information about:
◆ where the holidaymakers can travel to
◆ what they might experience
◆ what dangers they might face.

# ◼ Digging it up

This quarry used to be fields where farmers grew wheat and barley. The company started quarrying here ten years ago. We dig out slate. Some of it is used in local buildings, but most of it travels a long way from here.

If you dig down underneath your garden, town or the countryside, you eventually find solid rock under the soil. There are many different types of rock, all with different properties. We use many of these rocks to make our buildings, roads and jewellery.

**1** Survey your school buildings and grounds. Make a list of as many uses of rocks as you can find.

**2** Divide your list of uses into:
◆ uses that only change the shape of the rock
◆ uses that change the rock into a different substance.
What makes each rock suitable for its use?

**3** When the quarry company have taken all the slate they need, the site will be used as landfill and then returned to its original use. What do you think this means?

# ■ Why do we need rocks?

**Minerals** and rocks provide us with valuable chemicals. We use **ores** to give us metals such as iron and tin. We find diamonds and rubies and other gemstones in some types of rock. Other rocks are used as building stone, or to make bricks. Some rocks are even **chemically changed** to make substances like bricks, glass and rockwool.

> We made 3 256 000 000 bricks from clay in Britain in 1995.

## Production figures for some rocks and minerals in Britain in 1995

| Rock/mineral | How much did we produce in 1995? (tonnes) | What did we use it for? |
| --- | --- | --- |
| limestone | 90 933 000 | building and chemicals |
| china clay | 13 930 000 | china, such as mugs and plates |
| iron ore | 2 000 | iron metal |
| tin ore | 2 000 | tin metal |
| slate | 275 000 | roof slates |
| sand and gravel | 89 656 000 | building |

**1** In 1995, we bought another 18 670 000 tonnes of iron ore from other countries. Ten years ago, we mined most of our iron ore here. Why do you think things have changed?

**2** Find out how bricks are made. Why are bricks better for building homes than natural stone?

**3** Most of the world's valuable minerals are found in Africa and Australia. Find out which minerals are found there.

# Finding rocks

The Earth has a **crust** made from solid rock covered with either soil or water. Wherever you are on Earth, there is always solid rock underneath you. In the **mantle** and **outer core**, the rock is so hot that it is liquid or semi-solid. In the **inner core** the high pressure and temperature makes the rock solid.

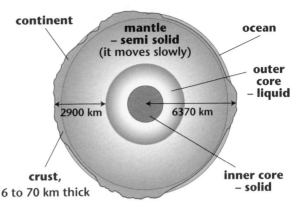

continent

mantle – semi solid (it moves slowly)

ocean

outer core – liquid

2900 km    6370 km

crust, 6 to 70 km thick

inner core – solid

# What are rocks?

▲ **Rocks** are mixtures of **minerals**. A mineral can be an **element** or a **compound**.

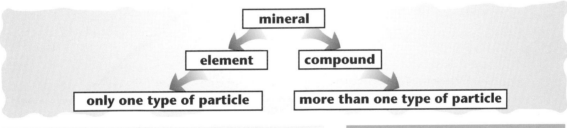

mineral

element

compound

only one type of particle

more than one type of particle

**4** Which of these are rocks and which are minerals?

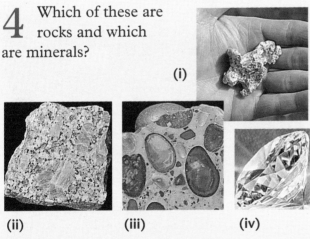

(i)

(ii)    (iii)    (iv)

**5** How do you think the rock in photo iii was made?

**6** How many different minerals can you see in photo iii?

## extra Early metals

**1** Gold is usually found as pure gold nuggets, not as compounds. Why?

**2** Why do you think that gold was one of the first metals to be used by humans even though it is rare?

**3** The mineral iron pyrites is called 'fool's gold' because it looks just like real gold. What methods could you use to tell the difference between fool's gold and real gold?

# Classifying rocks

> My job is to find the best places to look for minerals. It's not guesswork.
> We use **satellite** surveys to find the right types of rock. We take samples of rock from deep in the Earth and we look for clues. We know that certain minerals are found in or near certain types of rocks.

**Geologists** sort rocks into groups, just like biologists sort organisms into groups. This is called **classification**. Rocks are classified according to how they were made.

# Igneous rocks

Most of the rocks in the mantle and core are liquid or semi-solid. Rocks formed from molten rock are called **igneous rocks**.

**lava** flow – liquid rock or magma on the Earth's surface

layers of solidified **lava** make a **volcano** of **igneous** rock

magma

crust

fault

fault

crust

**magma** – hot liquid rock pushes up through fault

**1** The word igneous means 'fire' in Greek. Make a list of other words starting with 'ign' and give their meaning.

## investigation

### Lava flow

Lava may be at different temperatures and contain different substances.

How does temperature affect the thickness of lava? (You will use treacle instead of lava.)

Plan your investigation. How are you going to test for thickness?

Check your plan with your teacher then carry out your investigation.

When **magma** cools, it may form crystals. Some igneous rocks contain crystals that are valuable to us. A mining company might find diamond, emerald or ruby crystals deep inside a volcano. Crystals have regular patterns of particles. Other igneous rocks are glass-like. Glass rocks cooled so quickly that the particles did not have time to fall into a regular pattern.

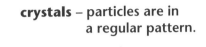

**crystals** – particles are in a regular pattern.

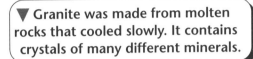

▼ Granite was made from molten rocks that cooled slowly. It contains crystals of many different minerals.

**glass** – particles are irregular.

▶ Basalt was made from fast cooling molten rock. It is a glass rock. Basalt is used for roads and for making rockwool and fibreglass. The Giant's Causeway in Northern Ireland is made from basalt. The basalt formed hexagonal columns when it cooled.

## *investigation*

### Crystals galore

Your teacher will give you a few drops of salol at 50 °C. Put a few drops onto a warm slide and a few drops onto a cold slide from the freezer.

Use a hand lens to watch the size of the crystal that forms.

What does this tell you about igneous rocks?

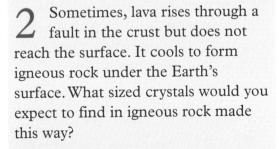

2 Sometimes, lava rises through a fault in the crust but does not reach the surface. It cools to form igneous rock under the Earth's surface. What sized crystals would you expect to find in igneous rock made this way?

3 Obsidian is a glassy rock. How do you think it formed?

# Sedimentary rocks

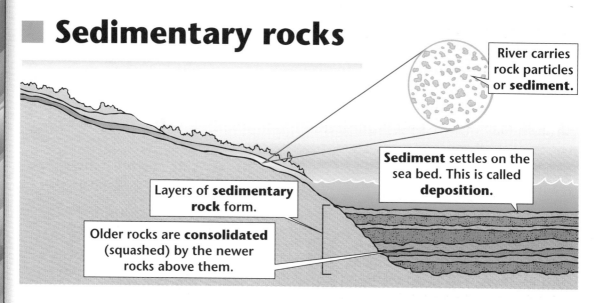

River carries rock particles or **sediment**.

**Sediment** settles on the sea bed. This is called **deposition**.

Layers of **sedimentary rock** form.

Older rocks are **consolidated** (squashed) by the newer rocks above them.

**Sedimentary rocks** are made when worn away particles of rock settle and then get stuck together. These processes are called **deposition** and **consolidation**.

Different sedimentary rocks are formed from different sized particles of rock.

## investigation

### Settling

Make a model river. How does the slope of your river affect the speed of the water?

What size of rock particle can your river carry at each speed? What happens to the rock particles when your river is level?

How does this help to explain how transportation and deposition happen?

| Particles | Particle diameter (mm) | What sedimentary rock does it make? |
|-----------|------------------------|-------------------------------------|
| clay | 0.002-0.0002 | makes mudstone |
| sand | 2.0-0.02 | makes sandstone |
| pebbles | over 2.0 | makes conglomerate |

Sedimentary rocks are softer and more crumbly than igneous rocks. Some sedimentary rocks were made from living things. Coal was made from layers of trees and ferns. Chalk was made from algae, and limestone from sea creatures. Other sedimentary rocks contain valuable minerals that were carried with the original rock particles.

▼ Sedimentary rocks can be crushed and sifted to extract valuable minerals such as tin.

4 Look at some samples of sedimentary rocks. What do you think are the characteristics of sedimentary rocks?

# Making fossils

Sometimes, a plant or animal is deposited along with the rock particles. The soft parts of the organism decay, but the harder parts remain and turn to rock as the sediment solidifies. The organism becomes a **fossil**.

▲ The seas that covered parts of the Britain millions of years ago were full of animals such as these ammonites. Many of their shells became fossilised in the sedimentary layers of chalk and limestone that were formed at the time. Ammonite fossils are common in many areas of Britain.

**5** Draw a picture or write an article to show what you think the ammonites in the photograph looked like when they were alive.

**6** Draw what you would expect the fossil of a snail to look like in a few million years' time.

**7** Fossil hunting can damage cliffs and the environment. Draw up a code of conduct for fossil hunters to safeguard the environment.

## extra  *Hard evidence*

We can use fossils to work out the age of sedimentary rocks. As the layers of sedimentary rock were being formed, remains of living things were fossilised in some layers. The sedimentary rock layers are the same age as the fossil remains. We could tell how old the fossils were because scientist have built up a **fossil record** showing what sorts of fossils were produced at different times. Until **radioactivity** was discovered, this was the main way of ageing rocks.

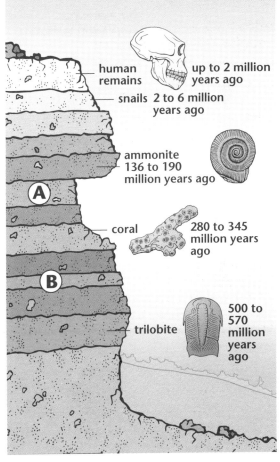

human remains — up to 2 million years ago

snails 2 to 6 million years ago

ammonite 136 to 190 million years ago

A

coral — 280 to 345 million years ago

B

trilobite — 500 to 570 million years ago

**1** Suggest when rocks A and B were formed.

**2** Research and write an article for a magazine to explain how the fossil record has been used to support the idea of evolution.

# Metamorphic rocks

The Earth's crust moves very slowly. As it moves, the rocks that make up the crust are pushed up and down and folded. Rocks can be pushed deep underground. As rock is pushed towards the centre of the Earth, the temperature rises and the **pressure** increases. The increased temperature and pressure can change the structure of the rock without melting it. The new rock is called a **metamorphic rock**.

Mudstone is a sedimentary rock. When it is heated under high pressure, it becomes a metamorphic rock called slate. All the particles line up in the same direction. This is why many metamorphic rocks are striped. Limestone forms the metamorphic rock marble. The particles in marble make a completely different pattern to the particles in limestone.

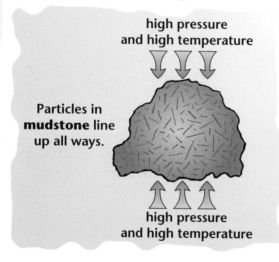

high pressure
and high temperature

Particles in
**mudstone** line
up all ways.

high pressure
and high temperature

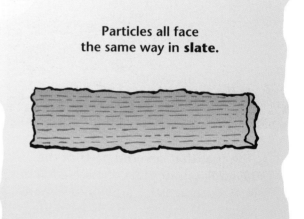

Particles all face
the same way in **slate**.

▼ Slate is a metamorphic rock; it is much harder and more brittle than the mudstone that it was made from. Slate can be split into thin sheets which we use for roofing.

8 Where in the Earth's crust can metamorphic rocks form?

9 How can you tell the difference between a sedimentary rock and a metamorphic rock?

10 Soapstone is a soft rock that can be carved to make bowls and ornaments. It is also used to make talcum powder. Do you think that soapstone is igneous, sedimentary or metamorphic? Why?

# Recycled rocks

Over millions of years, igneous, sedimentary and metamorphic rocks are **recycled**.

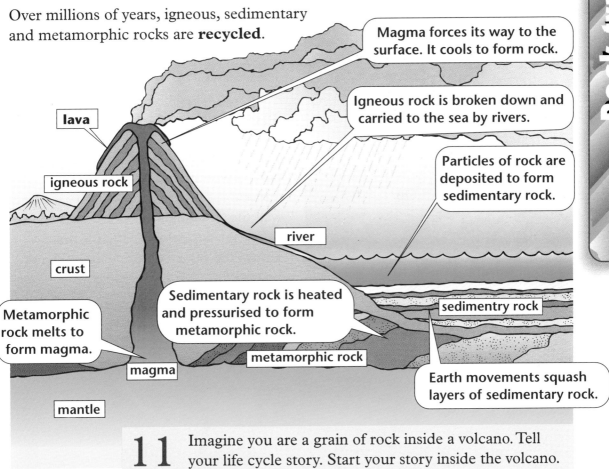

Magma forces its way to the surface. It cools to form rock.

Igneous rock is broken down and carried to the sea by rivers.

Particles of rock are deposited to form sedimentary rock.

lava

igneous rock

river

crust

Metamorphic rock melts to form magma.

Sedimentary rock is heated and pressurised to form metamorphic rock.

sedimentry rock

magma

metamorphic rock

Earth movements squash layers of sedimentary rock.

mantle

11 Imagine you are a grain of rock inside a volcano. Tell your life cycle story. Start your story inside the volcano.

## extra  *Deep sea mining*

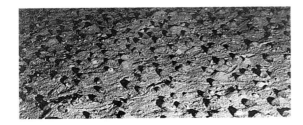

▲ Nodules of manganese on the ocean floor.

There are a lot of minerals in the oceans and seas. Some are dissolved in sea water, including small amounts of gold and silver. About fifty years ago, mining companies started exploring the ocean floor. They found a layer of nodules containing the metals iron, manganese, copper, nickel and cobalt. The nodules formed from sediments deposited by the oceans. These nodules can be used to obtain the pure metals. Nodules have been found in all the world's oceans, but the best nodules are in the Pacific Ocean.

1 We have deposits of iron and other metals under dry land. Why do mining companies need to explore the ocean floor as well?

2 Use diagrams to explain the type of apparatus you think miners use to mine the ocean floor.

39

# ■ Give us a clue

> We use two basic tests to help identify rocks and minerals in the field.

## The streak test

This test shows the colour of the powdered mineral. A sample of the mineral is scraped across the back of a wall tile (the unglazed side). This leaves some powder behind which is not always the same colour as the mineral.

## The hardness test

This test measures how easy it is to scratch a mineral.

| Hardness scale | Scratched by | Example |
| --- | --- | --- |
| 1 | fingernail (easy) | soapstone |
| 2 | fingernail | gypsum |
| 3 | copper coin (2p) | calcite |
| 4 | penknife blade (easy) | fluorite |
| 5 | penknife blade | apatite |
| 6 | steel file (easy) | orthoclase |
| 7 | steel file | quartz |
| 8 | steel file (difficult) | topaz |
| 9 | steel file (very difficult) | corundum |
| 10 | scratches every other substance | diamond |

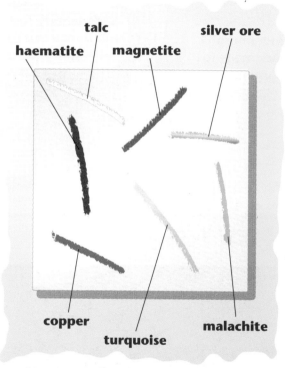

haematite talc magnetite silver ore

copper turquoise malachite

## investigation

### Investigating rocks

Test the rock samples you are given using the hardness test and the streak test. Try to identify all of the rock samples.

Divide the samples into three groups: igneous rocks, sedimentary rocks and metamorphic rocks.

# Making soil

> ▶ The type of soil in an area depends upon the rock underneath. Different rocks produce different soils.

We do not usually see rocks on the surface of the Earth. We see **soil**. Soil is made from very small fragments of rock held together by **humus**, the decayed remains of plants and animals. Different types of rock make very different soils.

The process of wearing down rock by wind and water to make soil is called **weathering**. The weathered particles are carried elsewhere by the wind and water, and often wear away other rocks. This is called **erosion**.

## Development threatens chalk downland

The planned housing estate west of Littleborough will destroy an area of chalk downland. This area is one of only a few left in the country with chalky soil, formed because the underlying rock is chalk. Chalk Milkwort and Burnt orchid grow there. The Burnt orchid only grows in a few other places in Britain and its numbers are declining rapidly.

## Weathering by temperature change

Materials, including rocks and water, change size as they are heated and cooled. The diagram shows how these changes weather rocks.

**In cold weather**

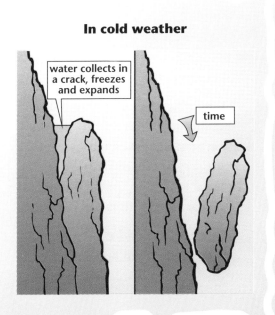

water collects in a crack, freezes and expands

time

**In deserts**

rock surface expands as it is heated, and contracts as it cools

day

the rock surface breaks up

night

1 Watch the effect of heating and cooling on a glass rod and a piece of chalk. Your teacher will demonstrate this for you. Describe what happens to the glass rod and the chalk. Can you explain why?

▲ Weathering and erosion have caused these odd rock structures in Goblin Valley, Utah.

## investigation

**Freeze force**

Investigate how much force freezing produces.

Check your plan with your teacher before carrying out your investigation.

2 What do you think is causing the weathering or erosion in each picture?

3 Why is more damage done to road surfaces in winter than in summer? What properties would road materials need to prevent this damage?

4 Make a key to classify igneous, sedimentary and metamorphic rocks. Remember, igneous rocks are hard with crystals, sedimentary rocks are soft and crumbly, and metamorphic rocks are hard and often have stripes.

5 The burnt orchid only grows on chalky soil. What special conditions do you think chalky soil provides for plants?

6 Make lists of the similarities and differences between a chalk rock and a chalky soil.

## investigation

**Weather it!**

Plan an investigation to find out if some rocks weather more easily than others.

## extra *How are caves made?*

These caves are in limestone rock. When the limestone rock was made, it was a solid lump of rock with no caves. Over hundreds of thousands of years, parts of the rock have been worn away to make the cave systems.

1 Make a list of suggestions for how these caves were made.

2 Plan and carry out an investigation to test your ideas.

- The Earth's crust is made of a layer of solid rock covered with a layer of soil or sea.

- Rocks are usually a mixture of minerals, although some contain one mineral only.

- Rocks are classified by how they formed.

- When molten rock cools, igneous rock forms.

- Igneous rocks are hard and some contain crystals.

- Sedimentary rocks are made from layers of rock particles deposited by rivers or the sea.

- Sedimentary rocks are softer and more crumbly than metamorphic and igneous rocks.

- Metamorphic rocks have been changed by heat and pressure.

- Metamorphic rocks are hard and some have lines or bands in them.

- Rocks are weathered by changes in temperature or by freezing water to make soil particles.

- Erosion happens when weathered rocks wear away other rocks.

**1** Copy and complete these notes. Use the words in the box to fill the spaces.

| pressure | molten | igneous | metamorphic |
|---|---|---|---|
| sedimentary | heat | classified | weathered |

Rocks are _____ according to how they were made.
When _____ rock cools,_____ rock is formed.
Small particles of igneous rock may be _____ and carried away by rivers. When the particles settle, layers of _____ rock form.
Rocks that are changed by _____ and _____ are called _____ rocks.

**2** What characteristics would you use to identify an igneous rock, a sedimentary rock and a metamorphic rock?

**3** Which rock types would you choose for each of the following tasks:
◆ carving a statue on a building
◆ making paving stones
◆ looking for gemstones in
◆ looking for fossils in?

**4** Draw a series of diagrams to show how a fossil forms.

**5** Explain how rocks are weathered and eroded on a beach. Give as many ways as you can.

**6** Make a list of six ways in which rocks can change.

**7** A yellow shiny mineral has a hardness of three and gives a gold streak. Can you name it?

**8** Pumice is an igneous rock with air holes like a sponge, and it floats on water. How do you think pumice was made?

**9** In several places in the world people live in houses built into caves in rock faces. Which rock type would you choose to carve out a cave house and why?

○ Make a list of the advantages of quarrying stone.
○ Think about jobs, money and the uses of the stone.
○ Make a list of the disadvantages of quarrying stone.
○ Think about the environment, noise pollution, other types of pollution, traffic and health issues.
○ Hold a public meeting to discuss the future of the quarry. Should the council renew its licence to quarry for another ten years?
○

# ■ Orchestral sounds

◀ Vanessa Mae is a famous violinist. She has learned to produce wonderful sounds by playing her violin in a carefully controlled way.

Few people listening to a concert will think about the processes that let them hear and enjoy the music. However, behind the scenes there are sound engineers who design the concert venues and sound systems so that the music sounds its best. They also help to record music and perhaps even design new instruments. All of these activities rely on what sound is and how it behaves.

**1** Hearing is one of your five senses. What are the other four? Why are your senses so important?

**2** Look around the room where you are sitting. Make a list of all the things that you could use to make sound.

**3** When someone plays a violin or guitar, how do they change the way they play to:
**a** make a high or low note?
**b** make a quiet or loud sound?

# ■ Good vibrations

**Sound waves** are caused by fast **vibrations**. Almost any object can make sound waves as long as the vibrations are fast enough and strong enough. Some musical instruments have large areas or strings that vibrate. When you speak or sing, your vocal cords vibrate. You can feel them vibrating if you rest a finger gently on your throat and make a quiet 'aaaah' sound.

The vibrations force air particles closer together, then further apart, then closer together. These 'squeezes' and 'stretches' are passed to air particles nearby and so the movement spreads out away from the source at about 340 metres per second. A **sound wave** is a series of squeezes and stretches.

Sound waves cannot pass through a **vacuum** because there are no particles to transmit the vibrations.

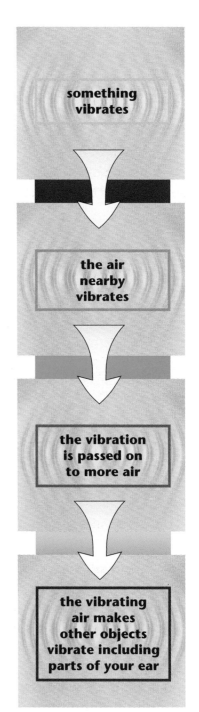

something vibrates

the air nearby vibrates

the vibration is passed on to more air

the vibrating air makes other objects vibrate including parts of your ear

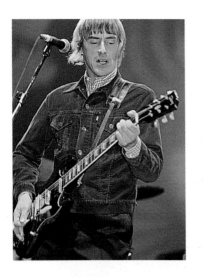

◀ These objects can all produce sound waves. As they move, they push the air close to them backwards and forwards. These air movements are sound waves.

1 Look at these pictures. What vibrates to make the sound in each picture?

# Loud or quiet

Loud noises are made by large vibrations. Large vibrations squeeze and stretch the air more than small vibrations.

As vibrations spread out, the number of air particles affected increases, so the **energy** of the sound is shared between more and more particles. The further the vibrations travel, the less the air gets stretched and squeezed, so sound waves become quieter as they move further from their source.

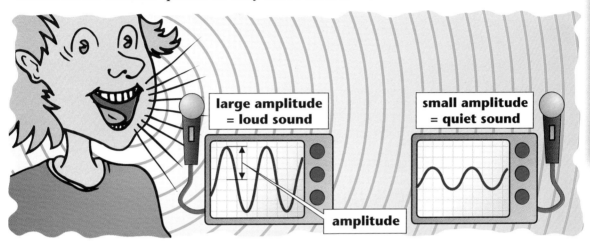

large amplitude = loud sound

small amplitude = quiet sound

amplitude

As the sound waves spread out the **amplitude** gets less. The sound is quieter. The number of vibrations each second, called **frequency**, is the same. Frequency is measured in vibrations each second or hertz (Hz). A sound of 1000 vibrations a second has a frequency of 1000 Hz.

**2** Each athlete on a race track has a speaker nearby. The speakers relay the sound of the starting pistol so that the runners know when to start.
**a** Why do the runners need speakers?
**b** Who would be affected the most if there were no speakers?

**3** The Round the World Yacht Race is started by firing a cannon from the shore. Do you think that this is a fair way of starting a race?

**4** Villagers are trying to stop a new airport runway being built near to their houses. They say the loud noise from the planes will damage their homes. Could their claim be true? Explain your answer.

**5** A snooper is using a glass against the wall to listen to his neighbours. Write the following statements in the correct order to describe what is happening.

> the vibrating wall makes the glass vibrate
>
> the sound waves make the wall vibrate
>
> sound waves spread across the room
>
> the snooper hears the sound
>
> the person next door talks
>
> the air is squeezed and stretched

# High or low?

Fast vibrations make sounds with a high **pitch**. Slow vibrations make sounds with a low pitch. Make an 'aaaah' sound starting with a note as low as you can make, and slowly make it higher. Hold your fingers to your throat to feel the vibrations as you change note.

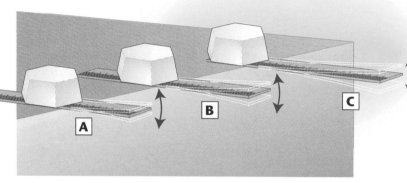

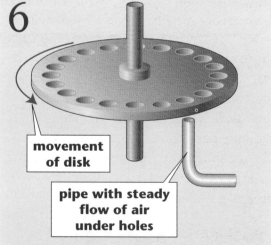

▲ The metal nails on this instrument vibrate at different rates when they are plucked. The shortest ones vibrate quickest and make the highest notes.

▲ Which ruler makes the fastest vibrations? Which one makes the note with the highest pitch?

If the vibrations are slow, less than 20 Hz, the sound waves that are made are too low for you to detect with your ears. Very slow sound waves can make you feel uncomfortable and quite sick. The police force is experimenting with using very low pitch sounds to control trouble-makers. The person the sound is aimed at cannot hear it but the vibrations stop them moving properly. Sound waves below 20 Hz are called **subsonics**.

If the vibrations are over 20 000 Hz, the pitch of the sound will be too high for you to hear, although dogs, cats and bats can. Sound waves above 20 000 Hz are called **ultrasonics**.

6

**movement of disk**

**pipe with steady flow of air under holes**

**a** Explain how pulses of sound are made using this siren.
**b** Explain why the pitch changes as the disk spins faster.

7 How could a drummer adjust a drum to make a higher pitched sound?

**8**

Which pipe will make the lowest notes? Explain how you made your choice.

**9** Elephants trumpet using their trunks. How will the pitch of the trumpeting change as an elephant grows larger. Explain your answer.

**10** A kidney stone could be removed by surgery, or by using the vibrations caused by ultrasonic. Which treatment do you think is better? Why?

**11** A manufacturer of a 'sonic clothes cleaner' claims that it is kinder to the environment than using detergent and hot water. Do you think such a claim can be true?

## Sound speed

Although we usually hear sound waves that have reached us through the air, sound waves can also pass through liquids and solids.

> ▶ Synchronised swimmers can keep in time with their music because sound waves travel through water just like they do in air. The vibrations travel faster through water, because the water particles are closer together than air particles.

Sound waves travel even faster through most hard solids because the particles in a solid are linked to each other. If one part is vibrated, the vibration is quickly passed on to other particles. Softer solids absorb some of the kinetic energy of the sound waves, so they are not as good at carrying sound.

Sounds cannot pass through a vacuum because there are no particles to pass on the vibrations.

| Material | Speed of sound (metres per second) |
|----------|-----------------------------------|
| air | 340 |
| cheese | 1300 |
| water | 1435 |
| steel | 5200 |
| Earth rock | 5000 |
| Moon rock | 1200 – 1500 |

**12** Order these materials to show how well they conduct sound, starting with the best. Gas, liquid, solid, vacuum.

**13** Is it true that sound travels at the same speed through cheese as it does through Moon rock? Explain your answer.

**49**

**14** Astronauts use radios to communicate. If they removed their helmets, they could not hear each other, even if they survived. Why not?

**15** People can feel animals stampeding before they hear them because of the ground vibrates. Explain why this happens.

**Sound ideas**

Some musical instruments produce sounds which are louder than others.

Carry out an investigation with members of your class who play instruments, to find out which ones are loudest and why.

## extra  *Which way?*

With two ears it is possible to work out which direction a sound has come from. As a sound from the side reaches your head, one ear detects it before the other. Your brain uses this to work out where the source is. Some animals can turn their ears. These animals can work out the direction more accurately than humans.

▶ The right ear of this owl is slightly lower than its left ear, and is tilted downwards. Its left ear is tilted upwards. The owl can also move its ears. These features help the owl to tell where sounds come from. An owl can catch a mouse in total darkness.

**1** Engines from large ships produce subsonics and whales communicate using subsonics. Conservationists think that this is why some whales lose their way and get washed up on beaches. How could you test this claim?

**2** At dawn, birds sing the 'dawn chorus' to claim their area. Each species sings its own special song.
**a** How can the song from one bird be different from the song of another bird?
**b** What does this information indicate about the hearing ability of birds?

**c** Suggest a kind way of testing whether or not a bird can tell the direction a sound has come from.

**3** Birds communicate through their songs. What other sounds do animals use to communicate with each other?

**4** Why is it useful for an animal to know which direction a sound has come from?

# ■ Reflections

If you shout at a tall building or a cliff you can hear your voice come back. The sound waves you made have bounced off the hard surface and come back to you, they have been **reflected**. This is called an **echo**. Soft surfaces do not make echoes, because they absorb the sound waves.

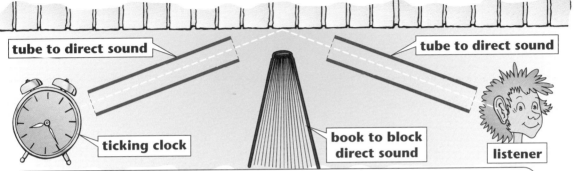

tube to direct sound

tube to direct sound

ticking clock

book to block direct sound

listener

▲ Reflection rules: you can prove that sound waves are reflected off at the same angle as they strike a surface by measuring the angles in this investigation.

One person makes regular sounds. Each time they hear the echo, they make another sound.

Another person times how long it takes for 10 sounds. They start when they hear the first hit, but don't count it.

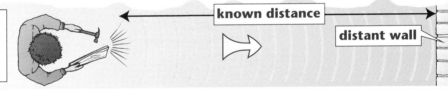

known distance

distant wall

reflected sound

▲ You can use echoes to find the speed of sound waves. You start timing the instant the sound is made and stop timing as soon as you hear the echo. If the timing is repeated you can use the average time to get a more accurate measurement. The speed of the waves is found using the relationship:

$$\text{wave speed} = \frac{(2 \times \text{distance to the place where the sound echoed})}{\text{average time measured}}$$

1 Salma used this formula to work out the speed of sound:

$$\text{Speed of sound} = \frac{(\text{distance to wall})}{\text{time for sound to return}}$$

Her result is very different from what the book says.
**a** What is the largest error in Salma's experiment?
**b** Make a list of any other errors in her experiment. Put them in order of importance.
**c** Suggest a better way for Salma to do her experiment.

# Using reflection

Reflections can be used to detect the distance and size of objects.

▲ The bat makes a short pulse of sound and measures the time it takes for an echo to return.

▲ The bat hears a fast but weak echo. It can tell that the object is close but small.

▲ The bat hears a slower but louder echo. It can tell that the object is further away but big.

▲ Bats use reflections to help them to find objects in their way, and their next meal!

Fishermen use pulses of sound to find shoals of fish, or to work out how deep the water is. **Ultrasound** can be used to test for cracks in materials because cracks reflect the ultrasound waves. Aeroplanes can be tested this way, without taking them apart first.

2 A ship transmits a pulse of ultrasound from its hull, to see how far below the sea bed is. It detects the returning pulse, 0.5 s later. What is the depth of the water?

3

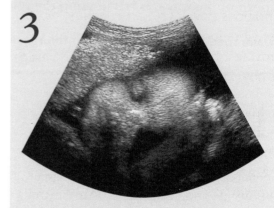

Ultrasound is used to see babies while they are still in their mothers' womb. Why might this be useful?

# Sound effects

Sounds made inside a room reflect off many surfaces. Your ears hear the real sound and all the echoes. The sound and the echoes overlap so your ears cannot separate them. Sounds last longer inside because it takes longer for the energy to be absorbed by the walls, floors and furniture.

This effect is called **reverberation**, and this the main reason why music made indoors seems different to music made outside. Music made in a cathedral reverberates for a long time because of the many hard surfaces. However, the same music made outside would not reverberate. Sound engineers design concert venues to alter the amount of reverberation so that the music sounds just right.

4

This person taps the ground and listens to the sound. Using these clues she can tell how far away the buildings are from her.

**a** How would the sound be different if she was walking by the side of a park rather than next to a building?
**b** How can she know if she is close to a building or far from it?

5 On a winter's morning, without getting up, you can tell that it has snowed just from the way the traffic sounds.
How and why is the sound different?

---

## extra  *Rock structures*

Seismologists are scientists who study the structure of the Earth by watching how vibrations travel through it. Seismologists use vibrations caused by earthquakes to provide information about the Earth, such as how large the molten core is.

To investigate rocks in a smaller area, seismologists have to make the rocks vibrate using small explosions. The seismologists then use instruments to listen to how the vibrations return from beneath the ground. They use the information to work out the shape of the rock formations.

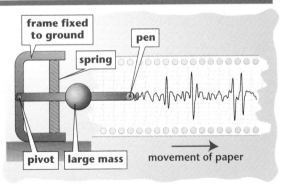

1 Why might knowledge about rock structures underground be useful?

2 **a** How might the test results from an explosion show there is a crack in a rock structure?
**b** How might the results be used to work out how deep the crack is?

# ■ Ears

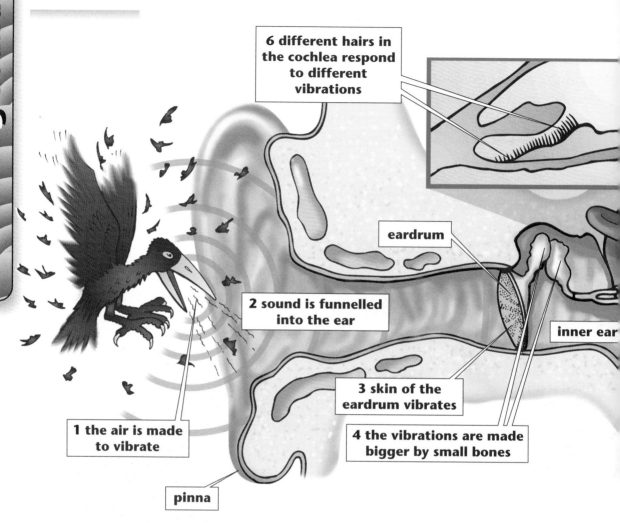

**6 different hairs in the cochlea respond to different vibrations**

**eardrum**

**2 sound is funnelled into the ear**

**inner ear**

**3 skin of the eardrum vibrates**

**1 the air is made to vibrate**

**4 the vibrations are made bigger by small bones**

**pinna**

**1** Use the diagram to find out which part of the ear does each of these jobs.

**a** catches as much of the air movement as possible and concentrates it into the ear

**b** turns the movement of the air into a movement of a small bone

**c** increases the amount of movement using levers

**d** turns the movement of the levers into the movement of a liquid

**e** turns the movement of liquid into an electrical signal to the brain

**2** Coral can be taken from coral reefs and carved into shape and used to repair the ears of some patients. Which parts of the ear could be repaired using this material.

# Ear problems

In some people the **eustachian tube** becomes blocked. Their **eardrum** cannot vibrate so they cannot hear. This is called glue ear. A small tube called a grommet can be fitted into the eardrum to let air move into the **inner ear** and help to keep the eustachian tube clear.

The eardrum can tear. This can happen with a bad ear infection, or if something sharp gets poked in. Doctors say not to put anything smaller than your elbow into your ear!

The hairs and sensors inside the **cochlea** can be damaged by infections. There are normally over 30 000 hairs, and any damage to them reduces your hearing. By the age of 65, you will have lost about 40 % of the hairs, especially the ones that detect high pitch sounds.

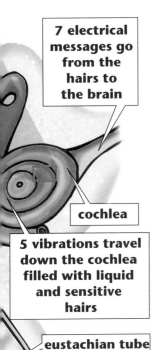

7 electrical messages go from the hairs to the brain

cochlea

5 vibrations travel down the cochlea filled with liquid and sensitive hairs

eustachian tube

3

In its day, this was the best sort of hearing aid there was. Work out how it improved a person's hearing.

4 Dolphins' ears don't stick out. Can you explain why?

5 Using your knowledge about how ears work, explain why everybody has a slightly different hearing range.

6 How and why does your hearing change as you get older?

7 Why might an old person find it more difficult to hear a child's voice than a man's?

## Investigation

### Where is it from?

Scientists claim that having two ears allows you to work out where a sound has come from.

Design an investigation to test this claim.

What data would you need to gather?

How would you handle the data to draw your conclusion?

# ■ Unwanted sounds

Your ears are delicate sensors and they are easily damaged by sounds below 4000 Hz. Listening to loud sounds is very dangerous. A sudden change in air pressure of just 0.001 % will cause permanent damage. If you are exposed to a loud noise, you should stay in a quiet place for at least 16 hours to give your ears time to recover. The Wellcome Trust estimate that about 18.5 million people in the UK are deaf or have severe hearing loss. That's about 1 person in 3!

Small amounts of energy can make very loud sound waves. The sound waves produced by a football crowd at Wembley stadium seem loud, but the total energy has been estimated to be only 5000 J; not enough energy to fry an egg.

In a French survey in 1996, one in five students who used personal stereos had a permanent hearing loss. The French Government has now passed a law which controls how loud the music on a personal stereo can be.

In the US military, severe hearing loss is the second most common reason why pilots are forced to retire early.

Pete Townsend was a famous guitarist with The Who, but he now suffers from severe hearing loss. Many rock musicians now wear earplugs to protect their ears. Should the audience wear earplugs too?

▲ Ear defenders should be used by people who do noisy jobs.

## investigation

### Save your ears

What features should a good pair of ear defenders have?

Design an investigation to find out which materials are best at stopping sound waves. Use your data to help you design the ideal ear defenders.

Whose design is the best?

8 In some areas people complain about hearing a quiet hum all the time. Some people say this is caused by powerful radar systems or the pumps that push gas through underground pipelines. How would you investigate the source of this noise?

9 In groups, discuss whether you think that noise is a type of pollution. What do you think should be done about people who produce nuisance noise?

## Using vibrations

▶ This aye-aye searches for grubs to eat by softly tapping wood with its long middle finger to find cavities inside it. The aye-aye can work out where the cavities are and if they contain grubs from the sound the tapping makes. If it thinks there are some grubs inside, it bites a hole into the cavity and uses its long finger to scoop them out. The aye-aye never makes a mistake.

▶ This spider can sense movement on its web. The caught bee is struggling which makes the web vibrate. When the spider detects a vibration it knows that dinner is ready!

Most animals can hear a wider range of sounds than humans, they can detect much lower sound and can pinpoint the source of the sound better than us.

| Creature | Typical hearing range (Hz) |
| --- | --- |
| human | 20 to 20 000 |
| cat | 20 to 25 000 |
| dog | 20 to 35 000 |
| mouse | up to 100 000 |
| bat | up to 120 000 |

1 A scientist claims that 'smaller animals hear higher notes'. Use the data in the table to argue for or against this claim.

2 Birds often stamp on the ground. Use the clues below to explain why.

Worms can sense vibrations.
Heavy rain makes vibrations in soil.
Worm skins need to be moist.
Birds eat worms.

3 Portia jumping spiders like to eat other spiders… even some twice their size. They can sneak up on their victims unnoticed, despite making the web vibrate. Scientists think that the vibrations they make are like those made by a falling twig, or a breeze so the victim is unaware that they are being hunted. Design an investigation to test this suggestion.

- Sound waves are made by vibrating objects.
- Fast vibrations make high pitched sounds.
- Large vibrations make loud sounds.
- Musical instruments can be adjusted to produce notes of different pitch and loudness.
- Sound waves need a material to travel through. They travel at different rates through different types of material.

- Sound waves cannot travel through a vacuum.
- Sound waves can change direction by being reflected.
- Sound waves spread out as they move away from their source.
- Our ears are easily damaged by large vibrations.
- Sound and vibrations have many uses in industry and research.
- Loud sounds can damage your health. Quiet sounds, over a long period, can also damage health.

## Questions

**1** Describe the difference in the movement of a string making a low note, and one making a high note.

**2** Explain why an orchestra sounds different at an open air concert to one inside a concert hall.

**3** At a large rock concert, some listeners notice that the lighting effects always seem to happen just before the sound changes. Listeners nearer the stage do not notice the effect. What is happening to cause the problem and is there a way to solve it?

**4** The composer Beethoven started to go deaf when he was 31. He was totally deaf by the age of 47. He carried on composing by resting the stick between the piano and his ear. He could sense the vibrations made when he played.
**a** Which parts of his ear might have been damaged to make him lose his hearing when he was only 31?
**b** Which parts of his ears still worked to let him to sense the vibrations for several years after this?

**5** Produce a poster to warn people in your school about the sound sources that can damage their hearing.

**6** An organiser of a rave says the loud noise doesn't cause permanent damage. He says the ravers soon recover their hearing after a rave. How would you respond to his claim?

## Investigate

**1** Hearing experts claim that if someone is going deaf the first sign is that they can't hear sounds of around 4 000 Hz.

They say that in later life the hearing of these people will get worse very quickly.

How could the evidence for this claim be gathered?

# ■ Looking after the planet

Most people think that a zoo keeper's job is just about looking after animals. However, a lot of my time is spent trying to get animals to breed and rear their young, and it doesn't always work. Understanding how organisms **reproduce** is vital to stop species becoming **extinct**. Some organisms, such as pandas, are only found in very small numbers in the wild, others can only be found in captivity. Zoos are important because we breed rare animals until there are enough of them to introduce back into their natural environment if it still exists.

**1** In groups, think of reasons why it is important to keep lots of different animals and plants alive?

**2** What is meant by extinction? What effects can the extinction of a species have on other organisms in the habitat?

**3** Find out the names of some plants and animals that are in danger of extinction. What is being done to save these organisms?

## Reproduction

# Differences

▼▶ In most animals it is easy to see a difference between males and females. Usually it is the male that has the brightest feathers or the loudest call. The reason for this is simple; males want to attract a female. By making themselves noticeable they are advertising themselves to females.

**1** Look carefully at the photographs of the animals above. Which one of each pair of animals do you think is the male? Give reasons for your answer.

**2** Can you think of any other reasons why the male in each picture might have these characteristics?

# Adolescence

At some stage a young animal has to change into an adult. Humans are no different from any other animal. Between the age of 13 to 15 most boys begin to change into men. This change is called **adolescence**, or **puberty**. Puberty usually starts earlier for girls; between the ages of 11 and 14. During puberty, your body develops features that show your sexual maturity. These are called **secondary sexual characteristics**.

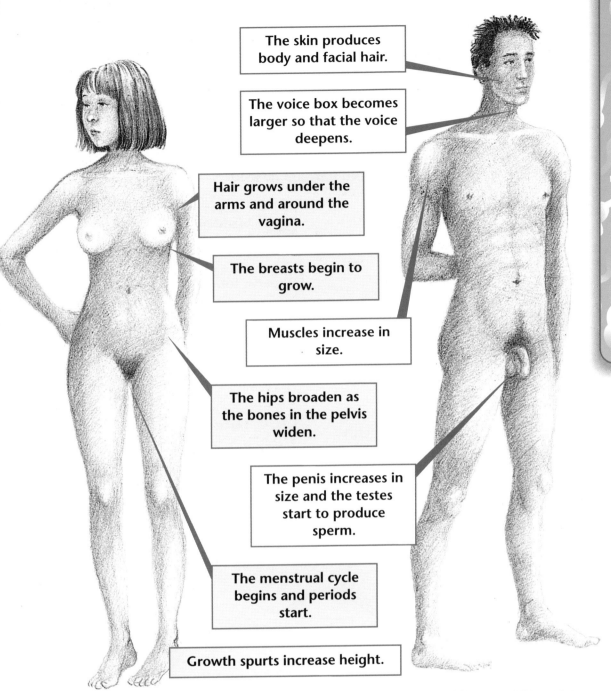

The skin produces body and facial hair.

The voice box becomes larger so that the voice deepens.

Hair grows under the arms and around the vagina.

The breasts begin to grow.

Muscles increase in size.

The hips broaden as the bones in the pelvis widen.

The penis increases in size and the testes start to produce sperm.

The menstrual cycle begins and periods start.

Growth spurts increase height.

Adolescence is started by **hormones** in your body. Hormones are chemical messengers that are carried around in your blood. Hormones control your physical and emotional changes. As an adolescent you often become more independent and less dependent on your family. Becoming an adult also means that you need to become more responsible. You often have little control over how you feel, but you need to learn to control the way you act.

3 List three similarities and three differences between the changes for girls and boys at puberty.

4 Carry out a survey of magazines to find out about the problems and worries that teenagers have.
**a** Are physical or emotional problems discussed the most?
**b** Write an imaginary reply to one of the letters giving advice to the teenager about their problem.

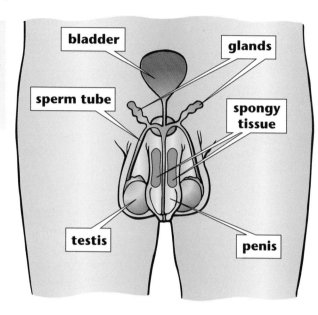

# Men

Male reproductive systems make and store **sex cells**. Men have two **testes** that make the male sex cells, called **sperm**. Together, the testes can make up to 250 million sperm every day! The testes store the sperm until they are needed.

5 How many sperm could a man's testes make in:
a one week
b one year
c his lifetime if he lives to 70?

The **penis** transfers sperm to a woman's **vagina**. This happens during **sexual intercourse**. Before intercourse, spongy tissue in the penis fills with blood; this makes the penis stiff, or erect. During intercourse, muscles pump sperm from the testes, along the **sperm tube** and out of the penis. As this happens, the sperm are mixed with fluid from the glands that feeds them and helps them to move along.

0.1 mm

**tail** – used by the sperm to swim

**body** – provides energy for the tail

**head** – contains the nucleus with half the information to make a baby

▲ Sperm are specialised cells. Their job is to swim from the vagina of a female, through the **uterus** and into the **fallopian tubes** to find an **ovum**. Although they are very small, sperm are excellent swimmers. They swim by waving their tail. The head of each sperm contains the nucleus; this carries half of the information needed to make a baby.

6 Why do sperm contain only half the information required to make a baby?

7 Describe two ways in which sperm are specialised. How do these specialisations make the sperm good at its job?

# ■ Women

Feodor Vassilyer was a remarkable woman. She was a Russian peasant who lived more than two hundred years ago. During her life she gave birth to 16 pairs of twins, 7 sets of triplets and 4 sets of quadruplets. Not surprisingly, she holds the world record for the woman who has given birth to the most children.

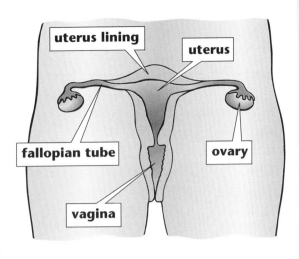

**8** How many children did Feodor Vassilyer give birth to?

**9** Different cultures and societies have different ideas about how many children a woman should have. Do you think that it is a good idea to have lots of children? Why? Discuss your answers as a class.

The female reproductive system lies underneath a woman's belly button. The two **ovaries** contain thousands of partly formed eggs, called **ova**. The **fallopian tubes** lead from the ovaries to the **uterus**, a muscular bag where a baby can grow. At the bottom of the uterus there is an opening, leading to the **vagina** and the outside world.

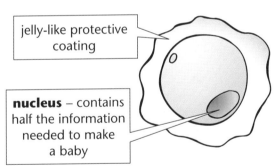

jelly-like protective coating

**nucleus** – contains half the information needed to make a baby

◀ An **ovum** is the largest human cell. It is about the size of a full stop. It has a jelly-like coating to protect it. Like sperm, ova have a nucleus that contains half the information needed to make a baby.

**10** Describe two ways in which ova are specialised. Explain why the specialisations make the cell better at its job.

**11** This photograph shows some cells from the wall of a fallopian tube. The job of these cells is to move the ovum along the fallopian tube. How are these cells specialised to do this?

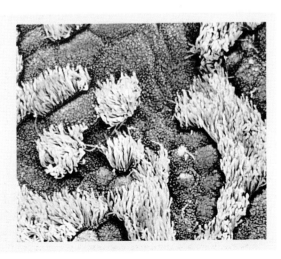

# Menstruation

At adolescence, the ovaries start to release one fully developed ova roughly every four weeks. This is called **ovulation**. The ovum travels down the fallopian tubes towards the uterus. Before ovulation, the walls of the uterus thicken with a new lining.

If the ovum is fertilised it attaches itself to the lining of the uterus. If the ovum is not fertilised, the uterus lining is not needed and is released. This produces a monthly bleeding called a **period**, or **menstruation**. The bleeding lasts for about 5 days, after which the whole cycle starts again.

When girls start to menstruate, their periods are irregular. It often take several years before the cycle becomes regular.

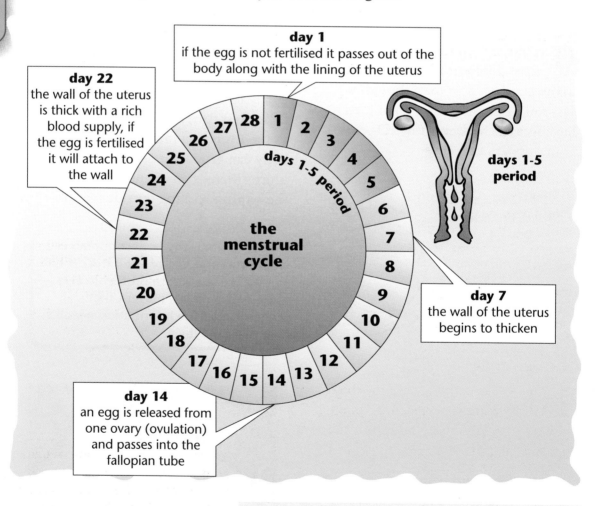

**day 1**
if the egg is not fertilised it passes out of the body along with the lining of the uterus

**day 22**
the wall of the uterus is thick with a rich blood supply, if the egg is fertilised it will attach to the wall

days 1-5 period

the menstrual cycle

days 1-5 period

**day 7**
the wall of the uterus begins to thicken

**day 14**
an egg is released from one ovary (ovulation) and passes into the fallopian tube

**12** Draw your own summary diagram to show what happens during the menstrual cycle.

**13** A girl starts her period on the 17th July. What day will it be when:
a her period ends
b ovulation happens
c her next period starts?

# Making a baby

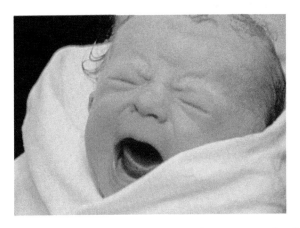

◀ When Louise Brown was born in 1978, she was the world's first 'test tube' baby. Doctors had taken an ovum from Louise's mother and mixed it with her father's sperm. The ovum was **fertilised** and put back into her mother's uterus. Then, just like every other baby, Louise grew in her mother's uterus until she was born nine months later.

The technique used to produce test tube babies shows how easy it is to make a baby. If sperm meet an ovum, they will fertilise it. The fertilised ovum can then grow into a baby. But, most children are not test tube babies. When a couple want to have a baby they have **sexual intercourse**.

Sexual intercourse is often called 'having sex' or 'making love'.

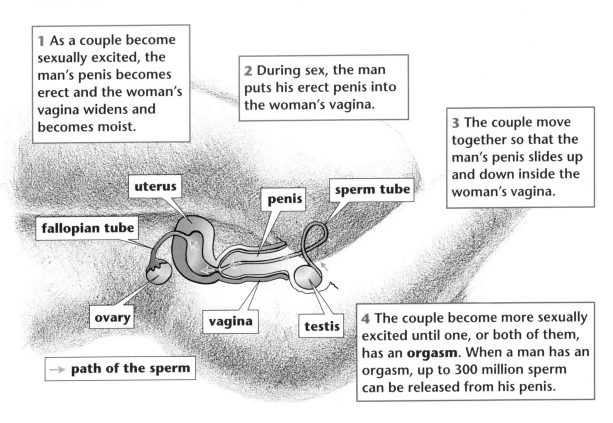

**1** As a couple become sexually excited, the man's penis becomes erect and the woman's vagina widens and becomes moist.

**2** During sex, the man puts his erect penis into the woman's vagina.

**3** The couple move together so that the man's penis slides up and down inside the woman's vagina.

uterus

fallopian tube

penis

sperm tube

ovary

vagina

testis

→ path of the sperm

**4** The couple become more sexually excited until one, or both of them, has an **orgasm**. When a man has an orgasm, up to 300 million sperm can be released from his penis.

1 Why do men release so many sperm when a woman only releases one ovum at a time?

## The great egg race

After sex, the sperm swim into the uterus and up the fallopian tubes. If there is an ovum in one of the fallopian tubes a sperm will fertilise it. Of all the sperm released, only about 100 will make it to the ovum in the fallopian tube. Only one sperm can fertilise an ovum.

2 Explain why a baby is not made every time a man and a woman have sex.

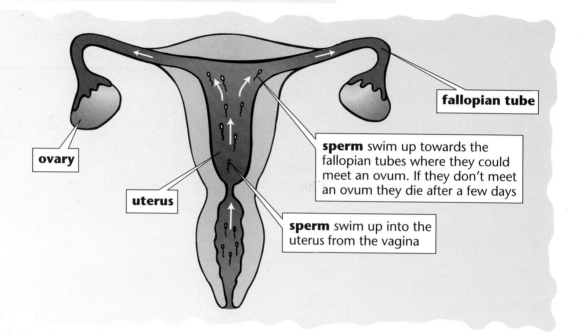

**fallopian tube**

**sperm** swim up towards the fallopian tubes where they could meet an ovum. If they don't meet an ovum they die after a few days

**ovary**

**uterus**

**sperm** swim up into the uterus from the vagina

## Fertilisation

Sperm will surround an ovum if there is one in the fallopian tubes. They press against the ovum, head first. Eventually one sperm breaks through the ovum membrane and its head enters the ovum. When this happens, the membrane hardens to keep out other sperm. The sperm nucleus then fuses with the ovum nucleus, this is **fertilisation**. The single cell that is formed has all the information needed to make a baby.

3 A sperm's head contains enzymes that break down cell membranes. Explain why sperm need these enzymes.

4 In your own words, describe the journey of a sperm, from the time it leaves a testis until it fertilises an ovum. Include the names of the organs involved and explain their function.

5 What is the difference between the way in which an ovum for a test tube baby and an ordinary baby are fertilised?

# Pregnancy

Two and a half thousand years ago, the philosopher Aristotle opened hen's eggs at different times after they had been laid in order to find out how chicks developed.

> ▶ In the Nineteenth Century, scientists such as Ernst Haekel formed a better understanding of how ova developed into different animals.
> He also discovered that as ova develop they look very alike.

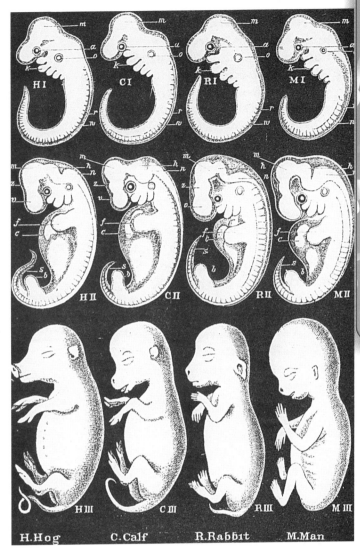

Today, we know much more about how ova grow and develop. The fertilised ovum starts to divide and becomes an **embryo**. In humans, this tiny ball of cells travels down the fallopian tube towards the uterus. Once there, the embryo attaches itself to the uterus lining. The uterus lining has a rich blood supply. It is the mother's blood that supplies all of the food and oxygen that a developing embryo needs.

6 Do you think that the pictures of embryos above look similar? What do you think the reaction to these pictures would have been in the Nineteenth Century, when most people didn't believe that humans could be related to other animals?

7 The embryos of some animals, such as birds, develop inside an egg shell outside their mother's body. Where do you think bird embryos get their food and oxygen from?

## The placenta

Soon after the embryo attaches to the uterus lining it develops a **placenta**. The placenta is a spongy mass of tissue that joins the embryo to the uterus. In the placenta, the blood systems of the mother and embryo come very close together so that materials can be passed from one to the other. The embryo's blood reaches the placenta through the **umbilical cord**.

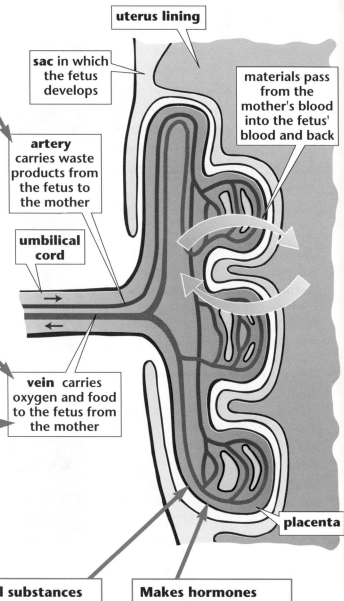

**Carries away carbon dioxide and other waste products**
Carbon dioxide is a waste product which your body gets rid of when you breathe out. The embryo cannot breathe out, so carbon dioxide and other waste products from the embryo pass across the placenta into the mother's blood.

**Provides food**
The embryo cannot eat, so it gets its food from its mother's blood. When the mother eats, food molecules pass into her blood. The food then passes across the placenta to be used by the embryo. It is important for a pregnant woman to have a good diet because she really is eating for two.

**Provides oxygen**
You need oxygen to stay alive. When you breathe, oxygen passes into your blood. The oxygen in the blood of the mother passes across the placenta to supply the embryo.

**uterus lining**

**sac** in which the fetus develops

**materials pass from the mother's blood into the fetus' blood and back**

**artery** carries waste products from the fetus to the mother

**umbilical cord**

**vein** carries oxygen and food to the fetus from the mother

**placenta**

**Protects the embryo from harmful substances**
The placenta acts as a barrier to many germs and drugs in the mother's blood. There are a few viruses and drugs that can pass across the placenta and can harm the embryo. The embryo is protected from some diseases by **antibodies** which pass across the placenta from the mother's blood.

**Makes hormones**
The placenta makes hormones to control the pregnancy.

8 Explain why pregnant women should not smoke or drink alcohol.

9 Why do pregnant women need to eat more food than they usually do?

After two months the human embryo is called a **fetus**. It has grown bigger and its cells start to specialise to do particular jobs. Some cells become muscle cells, some become nerve cells, and so on.

# Birth

The fetus grows and develops in the uterus. About nine months after fertilisation, muscles in the wall of the uterus start to contract. These **contractions** release the fluid that surrounds and supports the baby. The muscles push the baby, head first, through the vagina, and out of the mother's body.

Once it is born, the baby takes its first breath and blood circulates around its lungs. Soon after, the placenta is pushed out of the uterus, this is called the **afterbirth**.

10 Explain why the walls of the uterus are very muscular.

## extra Twins

Twins happen about once in every eighty pregnancies. Twins can be identical or non-identical. Identical twins are formed when a fertilised ovum splits into two completely separate cells. Each cell grows into a separate baby. As the babies originally came from the same cell they will be the same sex and look the same.

Non-identical twins happen more often. They are formed when two ova are released and fertilised at the same time. The babies that grow from these fertilised ova may not be the same sex and will look no more alike than other brothers and sisters.

1 Infertility treatments often involve giving women drugs to make their ovaries release lots of ova at once. Today, we see more twins because of infertility treatments. Can you explain why?

2 If twins were born as a result of infertility treatment, would you expect them to be identical or non-identical? Explain your answer.

3 Why do you think that triplets and quadruplets are much rarer than twins?

# ■ Plant parents

Everyone who comes into my shop loves the beautiful shape, colour and smell of flowers. But plants do not produce flowers to give us pleasure. A flower is actually the reproductive organ of a plant. Different plants produce flowers in a whole range of sizes, shapes and colours and at different times of the year. This is because plants reproduce in lots of different ways. It also means that I have lots of flowers to sell all year round.

Each part of a flower has its own special job to do. Most plants have flowers which make male and female sex cells. The male sex cells are found in **pollen grains** and the female sex cells are found in **ovules**.

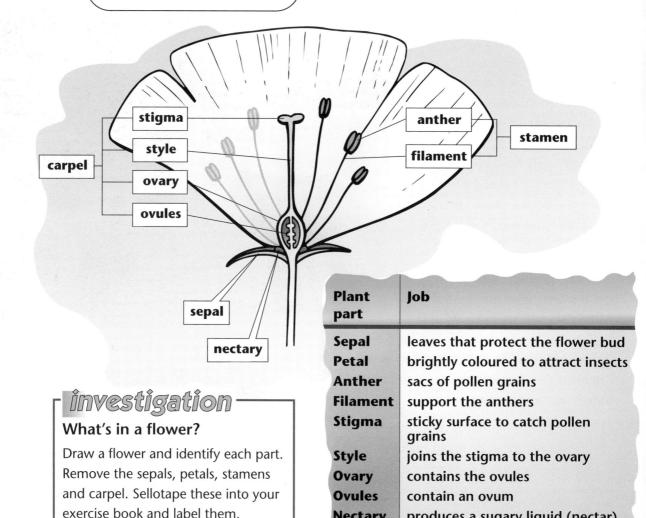

| Plant part | Job |
|---|---|
| Sepal | leaves that protect the flower bud |
| Petal | brightly coloured to attract insects |
| Anther | sacs of pollen grains |
| Filament | support the anthers |
| Stigma | sticky surface to catch pollen grains |
| Style | joins the stigma to the ovary |
| Ovary | contains the ovules |
| Ovules | contain an ovum |
| Nectary | produces a sugary liquid (nectar) |

## investigation

### What's in a flower?

Draw a flower and identify each part. Remove the sepals, petals, stamens and carpel. Sellotape these into your exercise book and label them.

# ■ Pollination

Pollination is the first step in plant reproduction. Pollen is transferred from the anther of one flower to the stigma of another. Different plants are pollinated in different ways.

▲ The smell and colour of flowers attract insects such as bees. The bee climbs inside the flower to feed on nectar and pollen. Pollen also rubs onto the bee.
When the bee enters another flower, some of the pollen that it has carried sticks to the stigma.

▼ Some birds drink nectar from flowers, and so pollen is rubbed onto the bird's head.
When the bird flies off to get nectar from another flower it rubs the pollen onto the stigma of the new flower.

▶ Some plants, such as grasses, are pollinated by wind. The anthers hang out the flower so that wind can blow the pollen to the stigma of another flower. Wind pollinated plants have small, dull flowers but they produce huge amounts of pollen.

## investigation

### Pollination in flowers

Study a selection of flowers or photographs of flowers and discuss how they might be pollinated. Which ones are insect pollinated and which are wind pollinated? Explain your answers.

1 Explain why insect pollinated flowers are brightly coloured and scented.

2 Plants that are pollinated by birds usually have large, brightly coloured flowers but no scent. What does this tell you about birds?

3 Many people are allergic to pollen and when they breathe it in they suffer from hay fever. Why does the pollen from insect pollinated plants rarely cause hay fever?

71

**Who pollinates who?**

Most flowers are pollinated by pollen from another flower of the same type. Some plants can also pollinate themselves. This is called **self-pollination**. The anthers and stigma mature at the same time. Pollen drops from the anther straight onto the stigma.

1 When do you think that it would be useful for a plant to be able to self-pollinate?

2 Carry out some to research to find out if there are any disadvantages to self-pollination.

3 Why do you think that the anthers and stigma need to mature at the same time for self-pollination to happen?

# Fertilisation

When flowering plants have been pollinated the male and female sex cells are still separate. The male sex cells are inside the pollen grains on the stigma. The female sex cells are in the **ovules** in the **ovary**.

For **fertilisation** to happen the male and female sex cells need to meet and fuse.

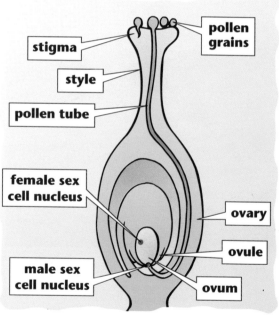

stigma
style
pollen tube
pollen grains
female sex cell nucleus
ovary
ovule
male sex cell nucleus
ovum

◀ After a pollen grain (yellow) lands on a stigma (pink), it grows a very fine tube, called a **pollen tube**, down the style to the ovary. A male nucleus travels down the tube to fertilise an ovum in an ovule. This picture shows a pollen tube growing, it was taken using a very high powered-microscope.

4 Why do plants need to be pollinated before they can be fertilised?

5 Why do pollen grains need to grow a tube down to the ovary in order for fertilisation to take place?

# Seeds and fruits

After fertilisation the ovules develop into **seeds**. The seed actually contains the plant embryo and all the food that it needs during early growth.

The ovary swells to make a **fruit**. Some fruits, such as plums, are fleshy while others, such as nuts, are dry and hard.

Plants provide us with oxygen, food, fuels, medicines and much more. But many environments are being destroyed and plants are threatened with extinction. At Kew Gardens we collect seeds from all over the world. Some of them are dried and frozen for storage. It is hoped that these seeds will last for hundreds of years so that in the future they can be used to grow plants that would otherwise be extinct. However, not all seeds can be stored like this. To save these plants, the seeds have to grow and reproduce. So it is really important to protect environments, because not all plants can be saved by just storing their seeds.

6 Why do the scientists at Kew dry and freeze the seeds before they store them?

7 Are plant seeds living or non-living? Explain your answer.

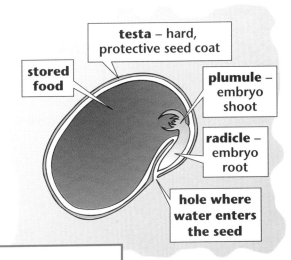

testa – hard, protective seed coat

stored food

plumule – embryo shoot

radicle – embryo root

hole where water enters the seed

## investigation

### Looking at seeds

Look at some seeds. Identify their testa, plumule and radicle.

# Scattering seeds

Plants cannot move, but by scattering their seeds their offspring can be spread far and wide. Plants scatter their seeds in many ways.

▲ **Seeds are scattered by animals when they eat fruit**
Juicy, sweet fruits are eaten by animals. The seeds are left behind in droppings which make an excellent fertiliser for the young plant.

▲ **Seeds are scattered by clinging onto animals' fur**
Some seeds have tiny hooks called burrs which stick to the fur of passing animals. When the animal grooms itself the seeds are dropped.

▲ **Seeds are scattered by the wind**
Propellers spin the seed away from the adult plant. Parachutes catch the wind and carry the seed away from the parent plant.

▲ **Seeds are carried by water**
Some trees have fruits that float. They grow close to water so that their seeds can be carried away.

▲ **Seeds are scattered by explosions**
Some seeds grow in pods. When it is dry, the pod bursts open and flicks out the seeds.

## investigation

**Seed and fruit circus**

Look at a variety of seeds and fruit and try to work out how each plant scatters its seeds.

8 Explain why a seed would not get enough water and light if it just fell to the ground.

9 Is a tomato a fruit or a vegetable? Explain your answer.

10 How do tomato plants scatter their seeds?

# Germination

Germination is the name given to the process where seeds begin to grow into new plants. Most seeds can survive for a year or more by becoming **dormant**. Seeds will only germinate when the conditions are right.

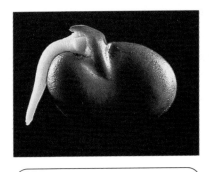

▲ **1** In warm conditions a seed takes in water. The water makes the seed swell and splits the testa.

▲ **2** The radicle begins to grow into a root using food stored in the seed. The new root grows fine root hairs which take in more water from the soil.

◄ **3** The plumule grows into a shoot. New leaves begin to grow on the shoot and produce food for the plant.

11 What conditions make seeds start to germinate?

- Boys and girls go through physical and emotional changes during adolescence.

- Sperm are adapted to swim by waving their tail.

- Ova are adapted to have a jelly-like protective coat.

- The menstrual cycle involves ovulation, the thickening of the uterus lining and the release of the uterus lining during a period.

- An ovum can be fertilised by sperm after sexual intercourse.

- A fertilised ovum can develop into a baby.

- The placenta supplies food and oxygen to the baby and removes carbon dioxide and other waste products.

- At birth, muscles in the uterus push the baby through the vagina, and out of the mother's body.

- Flowers are the reproductive organs of plants.

- Pollination is the transfer of pollen to a stigma. Most plants are wind or insect pollinated.

- On a stigma, a pollen grain grows a pollen tube, down which a male nucleus travels to fertilise an ovule inside the ovary.

- After fertilisation, ovules develop into seeds and ovaries form fruits.

- Plants disperse their seeds using animals, wind or water.

- Germination happens when a seed grows a root and shoot to make a new plant.

1 Write an article for a teenage magazine to explain the changes that boys and girls go through during adolescence.

2 Draw a poster to explain either what happens during the menstrual cycle or what happens to an ovum after it is fertilised.

3 Describe how sexual intercourse could lead to a baby being born.

4 Find an unusual flower. Draw your flower and label as many structures as you can. How do you think that your flower is pollinated? Give reasons for your answer.

5 Use diagrams to explain how insect pollination happens.

6 Draw a poster to show how a seed is formed and how it germinates.

1 Carry out research into endangered species in Britain. Present your findings as a letter to the Minister for the Environment urging the government to change their policies and suggesting ways in which we could help to conserve these species.

2 Investigate the conditions that different seeds need for germination. Gather data about:
- temperature needs
- light needs
- water needs
- soil needs.
Find the best way of presenting your data so that information can be found easily by scientists wanting to germinate seeds from seed stores.

# ■ Sports mad or mad sports?

The latest trend to hit the slopes is snowboarding. But, just like everything else in the world, it needs **energy** to happen. All the activities you can see around you need energy. I use energy when I wax my snowboard and when I ski with it. Energy is very important, without energy we would not be able to do anything.

**1** In pairs discuss:

◆ where snowboarders get their energy from
◆ how many different things snowboarders need their energy for.
Present your findings to the rest of your class. You could make a poster or give a presentation.

**2** For each of these activities state where the energy came from and what it is needed for.

Energy is transferring around and inside you all the time. But you only notice energy when something changes. Energy **transfers** in three main ways:
◆ as kinetic energy    ◆ as radiation energy    ◆ as potential energy.

# ■ Kinetic energy

The word kinetic means movement. So, **kinetic energy** is the energy found in moving objects or particles.

## Movement

▶ The moving drag car has kinetic energy. All moving objects have kinetic energy. This drag car has so much kinetic energy it needs a parachute to help it slow down.

## Sound

◀ Every year people are killed by **avalanches**. To help keep the mountain slopes safe, mountain rescue teams fire explosives into the snow. These explosions make the snow particles **vibrate**, carrying energy through the snow as sound. The sound vibrations make any loose snow fall.

Sounds can move through solids, liquids and gases. Sound travels by making particles vibrate, so it is a special sort of kinetic energy.

### *investigation*

**Sound waves**

Design an experiment to prove that sound can travel through solids, liquids and gases.

1 Do you think sound will travel faster through a solid, a liquid or a gas? Explain your answer.

2 Why do mountain rescue teams deliberately start avalanches? What time of day would be best to do this?

## Energy inside objects

▶ The energy in a hot drink helps to keep skiers warm. The energy of the drink comes from the kinetic energy of its vibrating particles – we feel this energy as 'heat'.

hot drink
fast vibrations

cool drink
slow vibrations

As an object gets hotter, its particles vibrate faster and the **temperature** of the object goes up. The higher the temperature the more kinetic energy the particles have.

As an object gets cooler, its particles slow down and energy is transferred to the area around the object. Energy always transfers from a hotter area to a cooler one. The bigger the temperature difference the faster the energy transfer.

It is difficult to find out exactly how much energy an object contains. The total energy in an object depends on:
◆ what the object is made from
◆ its mass
◆ its temperature.

The total amount of energy inside an object is its **internal energy**, sometimes this is called 'heat'. But heat is really the wrong word to use because it is a doing word, not a thing or an amount.

3 What sort of kinetic energy do the following have?

> a pop group singing
> a grasshopper jumping
> a burning fire
> a cup of coffee

4 For each pair, which will contain the most energy?
◆ a block of aluminium at 20 °C or the same block at 40 °C
◆ a 1 kg block of copper at 15 °C or a 1.5 kg block of copper at 15 °C
◆ a cup of water at 100 °C or a swimming pool full of water at 40 °C

# ■ Radiation energy

The Sun is a **luminous** object. Luminous objects are things that give out **radiation energy**. We see some of this energy as light, but there is more energy that we cannot see, this energy warms the Earth.

5 Which of the objects in the box are luminous?

> a star      the Moon      a mirror
> a working torch      a lit candle
> the Sun      a chair

# ■ Potential energy

**Potential energy** is stored energy. When an object moves, its potential energy transfers to kinetic energy.

## Gravitational

When the bungee jumper is at the top of the bridge, she has **gravitational potential energy**. This energy is stored because she has climbed above the ground against the force of gravity.

Any object above the ground has gravitational potential energy. It has gravitational potential energy because the Earth pulls everything towards it with the force of gravity. The higher up the object is, the greater its stored gravitational potential energy.

## Elastic

Another type of potential energy is **elastic potential energy**. When a piece of elastic or a spring, such as the bungee rope, is stretched or squashed it has a store of elastic potential energy.

◀ Before she jumps a bungee jumper has gravitational potential energy.

▼ At the bottom of the jump, the stretched bungee rope has elastic potential energy.

6 What is gravitational potential energy?

7 Why do skiers need gravitational potential energy?

8 Who has the most potential energy, a skier halfway up the mountain or one that is on the top of the mountain?

9 List five objects that store elastic potential energy.

## investigation

**More stretch, more energy?**

Find out if there is a relationship between the stretch of an elastic band and the amount of elastic potential energy that it stores.

# Chemical

► The power boat uses chemical potential energy stored in petrol as its energy source.

Chemical stores are stores of potential energy. **Chemical potential energy** is found in all energy sources, such as batteries, food and fuels.

**10** Copy this table. Put the items from the box into the correct column. Then add three more examples of your own to each column.

| Gravitational potential energy | Elastic potential energy | Chemical potential energy |
|---|---|---|
| | | |

a sack of coal    a sky diver    a diver on the high board    a battery
a jack in the box    a climber at the top of a mountain    a loaded catapult

# ■ Electricity

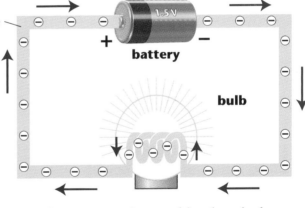

wire

direction of electric current

electrons move around the circuit, they have kinetic energy

battery

bulb

▼ This cable car uses electricity to get the energy to cross the glacier. **Electricity** is very useful. It can be used to do lots of different things because it is an easy way to move energy from one place to another.

The copper wire used in electrical **circuits** has moving particles called **electrons** in it. The battery creates an electric field that forces the electrons to move around the circuit. The electrons have potential energy before they start moving. Once they are moving they have kinetic energy.

**11** Why is electricity so useful?

**12** Draw a poster to teach young children about electricity and electric circuits.

# ■ Measuring energy

All energy is measured in joules (J) or kilojoules (kJ). 1 kJ = 1000 J.

Scientists can work out the energy content of a material by burning a sample with a known mass in a **bomb calorimeter**. The calorimeter records the temperature before and after burning. If you know how much material you started with you can then work out its energy content.

## Food energy

You get all your energy for living from food. Food contains chemical potential energy. All the food you eat comes from plants, or animals that feed on plants. Plants make their own food by **photosynthesis** using the Sun's energy.

BAKED BEANS
100 grams of Baked Beans
CONTAINS
5g protein, 14.4g carbohydrate
0.3g fat, 0.5g vitamins
and minerals, 5.4g fibre,
71.7g water
ENERGY VALUE = 330 kJ
= 79 kcal

▲ All foods have a label telling us what is in the food. The energy value is given in kilojoules and kilocalories. The calorie is an old unit for energy.

### investigation

**Energy foods**

Plan an experiment to measure the energy content of different of foods. Find out why some foods are better energy stores than others.

**13** Why do different people have different energy needs?

**14** Using the food label, calculate how many joules there are in a kilocalorie.

**15** We say that the Sun is the ultimate source of energy on Earth. Explain what this means. How do we trap the Sun's energy?

### extra *Extreme sports*

Extreme sports, such as white water canoeing, use the speed of energy transfers to make the sport really exciting. The faster the energy transfer the more thrilling the experience.

**1** What other sports use fast energy transfers to make them exciting?

**2** Carry out a survey to find out what sports people find scary but fun. Try to find out why some people enjoy being scared for fun but others do not.

# What is work?

> ► Cross country skiers work very hard and they use up a lot of energy. They transfer the potential energy stored in their muscles to kinetic energy when they ski. Not all the potential energy is transferred as kinetic energy, some is transferred to the surroundings and lost. The skier is an **energy transfer device**.

To make things happen we need to be able to transfer energy. Scientists have a special name for transferring energy. They call it **work**. Without energy you could not work. Work can mean a lot of different things. It can be listening to your favourite music, doing your homework, walking to school or going to the office. The more energy you have, the more work you can do.

chemical potential energy in muscles

kinetic energy + energy lost to surroundings as skier gets hotter

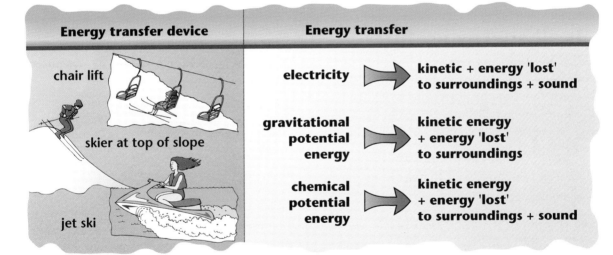

| Energy transfer device | Energy transfer |
|---|---|
| chair lift | electricity ➡ kinetic + energy 'lost' to surroundings + sound |
| skier at top of slope | gravitational potential energy ➡ kinetic energy + energy 'lost' to surroundings |
| jet ski | chemical potential energy ➡ kinetic energy + energy 'lost' to surroundings + sound |

1 How are energy and work linked?

2 What are the energy transfers for a climber climbing a rock face.

3 What are the energy transfers for a mountain biker coming down a mountain.

4 Which of these are energy transfer devices? What are the energy transfers for each energy transfer device.

> loudspeaker   speedboat   computer
> plastic cup   radio   pizza   ski pole

# ■ Conserve it

▶ Athletes need a good store of potential energy at the start of a marathon. During the race they transfer potential energy to kinetic energy, but they also lose energy to the air around them as they get hotter and hotter.

▶ This diagram shows what happens to every 100 J of energy the marathoner starts with. The size of the arrows shows how much energy transfers as each different form of energy. Diagrams like this are called **Sankey diagrams**.

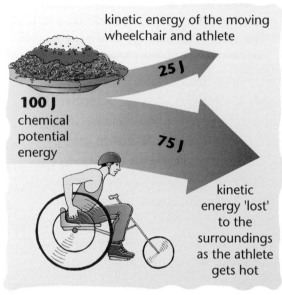

kinetic energy of the moving wheelchair and athlete

25 J

100 J chemical potential energy

75 J

kinetic energy 'lost' to the surroundings as the athlete gets hot

Whenever you transfer energy you always end up with the same amount that you started with. This is called the **Law of Conservation of Energy**. This Law tells us that energy is never created or destroyed, it is just transferred.

## Is all energy useful?

As energy transfers it is **dissipated**. Dissipated is the scientific word for spreading out. In every energy transfer some of the energy is lost to the surroundings. The more times the energy is transferred the more dissipated it becomes, and the less useful it is. But the total amount of energy always stays the same.

**5** What is the law of conservation of energy?

**6** A motor bike transfers 400 J of stored potential energy to 100 J of kinetic energy, 250 J of energy lost to the surroundings and 50 J of sound. Draw a Sankey diagram showing the energy transfers.

**7** Here is an energy transfer diagram for a jet ski.

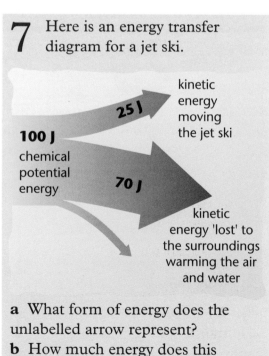

kinetic energy moving the jet ski

25 J

100 J chemical potential energy

70 J

kinetic energy 'lost' to the surroundings warming the air and water

**a** What form of energy does the unlabelled arrow represent?
**b** How much energy does this account for?

**8** Explain why energy is dissipated as it is transferred.

**9** This is Celeste's diary for one morning. Rewrite her diary to show the energy transfers that happened during Celeste's morning.

◆ turned alarm off at 7.00 am
◆ showered and dressed 7.10 am

◆ had breakfast 7.30 am
◆ left house for school at 8.15 am
◆ cycled 0.8 km along road to bus stop to meet Sally, walked up the hill to school chatting to Sally
◆ arrived at school 8.40 am

## extra  *Energy Efficiency*

Car manufacturers often talk about the **efficiency** of their cars. But what do they mean when they say 'more efficient'?

To scientists, efficiency is a measure of how much useful energy is transferred when work is being done by a **machine**. To car manufacturers, efficiency means how many kilometres the car will do per litre of fuel.

Efficiency can be calculated using this equation:

$$\% \text{ efficiency} = \frac{\text{useful energy transferred} \times 100}{\text{total energy at start}}$$

in the car above, $\% \text{ efficiency} = \dfrac{250 \times 100}{1000} = 25\%$

**1000 J** chemical potential energy

**250 J** — kinetic energy moving the car

**750 J** — energy 'lost' to surroundings as the car heats up + sound

No machines are 100 % efficient because whenever energy is transferred some of it is dissipated to the surroundings as useless energy.

**1** A petrol engine is 25 % efficient. Explain what this means.

**2** For each machine in the table, name the energy source and draw a Sankey diagram to show what happens to each 100 J of the energy source.

| Machine | % Efficiency |
|---|---|
| petrol car engine | 25 |
| diesel car engine | 35 |
| human 'engine' | 20 |
| electric milk float motor | 80 |

**3** John has chosen a car he likes but he can't decide between the diesel model and the unleaded petrol model. He knows that diesel costs 61.8 pence per litre and unleaded petrol costs 61.6 pence per litre. Can you help him choose?

**4** New refrigerators are more efficient than older models, manufacturers say that they are 'environmentally friendly'. How they can make this claim?

**5** The cheetah is the fastest land animal. It can reach speeds of 110 km/ph. The cheetah has an efficiency of 15 %. Calculate how much energy it can use to run after a 6000 J meal.

# Conduction

Conduction happens when energy travels through a material.

If energy can move through a material easily we call the material a **conductor**. If energy can't move through a material easily we call the material an **insulator**.

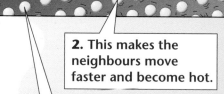

1. When solids heat up the particles at the hot end move around faster bumping into their neighbours.

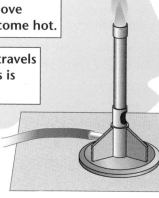

2. This makes the neighbours move faster and become hot.

3. In this way heat travels along the solid. This is called **conduction**.

▼ The bear's fur coat traps air to stop energy escaping by conduction. A ski suit works in just the same way, trapping warm air between the fibres.

## investigation

**Energy movers**

Design an investigation to find out which material is the best insulator for use in a ski suit. Test your insulator in cold, wet and windy conditions.

2 Why do metal ski poles feel cold to touch but the rubber handles feel warm?

3 When penguins get cold their feathers stand up. Explain how this helps to keep them warm.

4 When ski clothes are made they are tested for:

A  wear and tear
B  ability to keep out the wind
C  ability to keep out water
D  insulating properties

Using a scale of 1-10, where 10 is the best, award each test a number that you would expect from the clothes giving reasons for your choice.

1 Separate the items in the box into conductors and insulators.

> water   iron   aluminium
> wood   polystyrene
> air   copper

## extra *What makes a good insulator?*

> We get cold faster in water than in air because water is a better conductor than air. We use wetsuits made of a special air filled rubber, called neoprene. The tiny pockets of air slow down energy loss by conduction.

Materials conduct energy at different rates. The rate of energy transfer through a material is called its **thermal conductivity**. The higher the thermal conductivity, the faster energy transfers through the material.

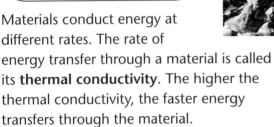

| Material | Thermal conductivity compared to glass |
|----------|----------------------------------------|
| air | 0.024 |
| water | 0.59 |
| iron | 80 |
| copper | 385 |

**1** Why do metals make the best conductors?

**2** Why is air a poor conductor of heat?

**3** Explain why neoprene is good at keeping divers warm.

**4** The most expensive saucepans have copper bases. Why?

## Convection

Most of the energy transferred from your body escapes from your head. Your head transfers energy by **convection**. Moving gas or liquid particles are needed for convection.

a **convection current**

cool air moves in to replace warm air

warm air rises

Cutting down the circulation of air particles reduces the amount of energy transferred. Materials that trap air, such as hair, fleece and fur, also help to slow down the energy transfer.

**5** What is a convection current?

**6** Why can't solids transfer energy by convection?

**7** Why is it sensible to wear a hat on a cold winters day? Why is a fleecy hat better than a cotton one?

**8** A fire in a room transfers energy to the room by convection. Draw a diagram to show how this happens.

## Radiation

The Earth is warm because it absorbs the Sun's **radiation**. There is empty space between Earth and the Sun. Unlike convection and conduction, radiation does not need moving particles to carry it.

Your body transfers energy by radiation all the time. All warm objects **emit** radiation. The hotter the object, the more energy it gives out. People who exercise get hot, they transfer more energy by radiation while they are exercising to cool down.

▶ These hot marathon runners emit lots of radiation at the end of the race. They use silver blankets to stop them cooling down too quickly.

## investigation

**Do silver blankets really work?**

Plan an investigation to see if silver blankets really do keep warm objects warmer for longer.

## Good and bad radiators

Some surfaces are better at emitting and absorbing heat radiation than others. Dull black surfaces are the best absorbers and emitters of radiation. They **reflect** hardly any radiation at all.

Shiny, silvery surfaces are the worst absorbers and emitters of radiation. They reflect nearly all the radiation that hits them.

**9** What is radiation?

**10** How do silver blankets stop marathon runners cooling too quickly at the end of a race?

**11** Who else might use silver blankets?

**12**

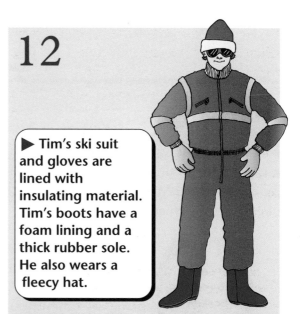

▶ Tim's ski suit and gloves are lined with insulating material. Tim's boots have a foam lining and a thick rubber sole. He also wears a fleecy hat.

For each of these features explain how they help to keep Tim warm.
◆ his hat
◆ the material used for his ski suit and gloves
◆ the light colourof his ski suit
◆ his boots

# ■ Body heat

Your body transfers energy to its surroundings by **conduction**, **convection** and **radiation**. Your body can also lose some energy by **evaporation**. All these different ways of moving energy can be useful if you want to keep cool but a problem if you want to stay warm.

> ▶ Emperor penguins breed in the South Pole. There is no shelter from the cold and snow blizzards. To keep warm and protect their young, the penguins huddle together and take it in turns to be on the outside. The cold makes their feathers stand up to trap a layer of air to help keep them warm.

Like a penguin, your body has a temperature control system that keeps you at a steady temperature. You need a core temperature of about 37 °C for your body to work properly.

If your core temperature falls to below 32 °C your muscles stop working and you stop shivering. This lowers your body temperature even further, leading to **hypothermia**. Your body will stop working properly and you could fall in to a coma and die. Overheating can be just as dangerous as over cooling.

**37° C**

**13** Explain how the narrowing of your blood vessels near your skin helps you to keep warm.

**14** How does your body stay cool on a hot day?

**15** How does panting help to cool a dog when it is hot?

> ◀ The core temperature for humans is 37 °C.

| blood vessels near the skin open wide so that warm blood can lose energy through the skin (vasodilation) | | blood vessels near the skin narrow keeping warm blood in the core (vasoconstriction) |

| sweating – sweat evaporates taking energy with it | hairs on body lie flat to let energy escape | body at 37° C | hairs on body stand up to trap layer of air for insulation | shivering muscles release energy to warm body |

**energy lost**

| body at more than 37° C | | body at less than 37°C |

- We need energy for everything that we do.

- All energy is either kinetic, potential or radiation energy.

- Kinetic energy is movement energy.

- Potential energy is stored energy.

- Energy is measured in joules (J) or kilojoules (kJ).

- To make use of energy we must be able to transfer it.

- Energy is never created or destroyed, it is just transferred.

- Energy is dissipated as it is transferred.

- Work is done when energy transfers.

- Insulation can be used to reduce energy transfer.

- Your body transfers energy using conduction, convection, radiation and evaporation.

1 Electricity and sound are both types of kinetic energy. Explain this statement.

2 What do scientists mean by 'work'?

3 What is the law of conservation of energy?

4 What happens to dissipated energy?

5 A skier takes in 250 kJ of energy. She transfers 50 kJ as kinetic energy, 180 kJ as energy lost to the surroundings and 20 kJ as sound energy. Draw an energy transfer diagram for the skier. Calculate her efficiency.

6 List all the examples of energy transfer by conduction, convection and radiation in your home.

7 Explain why a hot cup of tea cools down quickly to start with then more slowly as time passes.

8 Why is it wrong to say, "close the door or you will let the cold in"? What would be the correct thing to say?

When skiers ski down a mountain they transfer potential energy to kinetic energy and lose some energy to their surroundings.

The lost energy is produced by **friction** between the skis and snow and the air resistance between the skier and the air.

Investigate the factors that affect the speed at which skiers travel down a mountain.

THE BODY SHOP

> Many of our products contain natural ingredients based on traditional recipes. None of them have been tested on animals. Our Aloe Vera Body Lotion is a rich cream. It contains a mixture of aloe vera, shea butter, wheatgerm oil and apricot oil. We always mix the same proportions of each ingredient so that our cream is always the same.

## ■ What is it made from?

Making and selling cosmetic products is big business. But are the cosmetic products we use really that different from each other or are they just made from the same few ingredients mixed in different amounts, with different smells?

**1** Survey the ingredients list on as many cosmetic products as you can find. Look at shampoos, toothpastes, soaps, etc.
◆ Can you find any common ingredients?
◆ Try to find out the purpose of each ingredient.

◆ Which ingredients do you think are pure substances and which are mixtures?

**2** Find the best way of presenting your information about the ingredients used in these cosmetics.

**91**

# ■ A question of matter

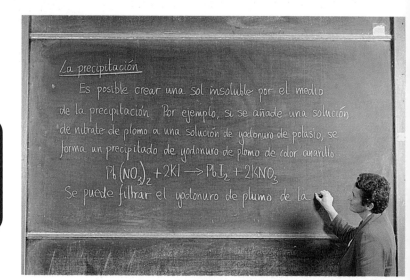

> ► Scientists all over the world need to talk to each other. They may speak different languages, but they all use the same chemical language.

Everything around you is made from tiny particles, called **atoms**. There are 92 different types of natural atoms. Substances made from only one type of atom are called **elements**. So, there are 92 natural elements.

Elements are the building blocks of everything around you.
◆ Hydrogen and oxygen are the elements that make water.
◆ Sodium and chlorine are the elements that make salt.
◆ Carbon, hydrogen and oxygen are the elements that make the oils in the Aloe Vera Body Lotion.

You will know the names of some elements, such as gold and oxygen. But, most people have never heard of the elements dysprosium and ytterbium. Scientists have given all elements a chemical name and a **chemical symbol**. Some chemical symbols are easy to work out from the element name, but others are very different to their names because they come from old Latin names.

| Element | Symbol | Reason |
|---------|--------|--------|
| carbon | C | the first letter of the name |
| calcium | Ca | the first two letters of the name |
| magnesium | Mg | the first and third letter of the name |
| iron | Fe | the Latin word for iron is ferrum |
| lead | Pb | the Latin word for lead is plumbum |
| sodium | Na | the Latin word for sodium is natrium |

**1** Find out what elements these symbols represent: Br, I, H, B and Au.

**2** Why is the symbol for calcium Ca and not C?

**3** You have discovered a new element. You are naming it after yourself. Give the element a symbol. Explain your choice of symbol.

# Body Chemicals

▶ Most of your body is made from just ten elements. A person with a mass of 50 kg will be made from these elements:

| Element | Amount (litres or grams) | What is it like when it is pure? |
| --- | --- | --- |
| hydrogen | 60 000 l | a very reactive gas |
| oxygen | 24 000 l | a gas |
| nitrogen | 1 300 l | a gas |
| chlorine | 25 l | a poisonous green gas |
| carbon | 9000 g | a black solid |
| calcium | 1000 g | a reactive metal |
| phosphorus | 500 g | a reactive solid used in matches |
| potassium | 200 g | a metal that burns in water |
| sulphur | 150 g | a yellow solid |
| sodium | 75 g | a metal that fizzes in water |

You do not look like a mixture of these elements. You do not contain patches of poisonous green gas or dangerous metals that burn in water. The substances that your body is made from are **compounds**. Compounds are made when atoms of different elements join together in a **chemical reaction**. The properties of a compound are usually very different to the properties of the elements it contains. A particle made from two or more atoms chemically joined together is called a **molecule**.

4 What is the difference between an element and a compound?

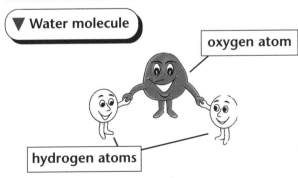

▼ Water molecule

oxygen atom

hydrogen atoms

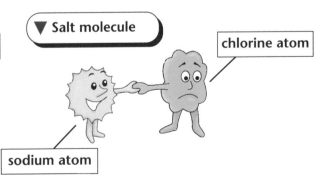

▼ Salt molecule

chlorine atom

sodium atom

Water is made from the elements hydrogen and oxygen.
There are two atoms of hydrogen and one atom of oxygen.
We write the formula for water as $H_2O$.
This is called its **chemical formula**.

Salt is made from the elements sodium and chlorine.
There is one atom of sodium and one atom of chlorine.
Its chemical formula is NaCl.

## Always the same?

Water is always made from two hydrogen particles and one oxygen particle. It makes no difference where or how the water was made. The number and types of atom in a compound are always the same. This is the **Law of Constant Composition**.

## All mixed up

Air is a **mixture**. It is made from oxygen, nitrogen, carbon dioxide, neon, argon and water. The amount of water in the air changes with the weather. The amount of carbon dioxide changes with the number of plants and factories. You cannot write a formula for air or any other mixture.

▶ Plants use carbon dioxide during **photosynthesis**. Some industries release carbon dioxide into the air as a waste product. So, the proportion of carbon dioxide in the air varies from place to place.

**5** Write chemical formulae for these molecules.

**6** Why do you think that the amount of carbon dioxide in the air in a rain forest and around a factory are different? Which area will have a higher level of carbon dioxide?

**7** Look at these diagrams. Draw a similar diagram to show a mixture of an element and a compound.

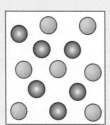
**a mixture of two elements**

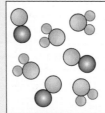
**a mixture of two compounds**

**8** Which are mixtures and which are compounds?

> orange squash   toothpaste   carbon dioxide
> wine   vinegar   copper sulphate   salt   cake

**9** Sea water is a mixture.

**a** How does its composition change around the world?
**b** How could you separate the substances in sea water?

**10** Is it more difficult to predict what happens when you react a chemical with a mixture or with a pure substance? Why?

# Element, compound, mixture?

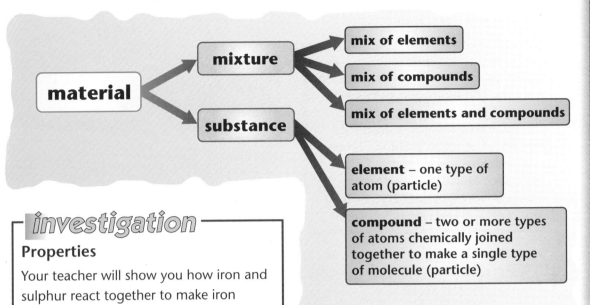

material → mixture → mix of elements / mix of compounds / mix of elements and compounds

material → substance → element – one type of atom (particle) / compound – two or more types of atoms chemically joined together to make a single type of molecule (particle)

## investigation

**Properties**

Your teacher will show you how iron and sulphur react together to make iron sulphide. Investigate the properties of:

a  iron

b  sulphur

c  a mixture of iron and sulphur

d  iron sulphide.

**11** Design a system to separate a mixture of iron filings and sulphur powder. Draw a poster to show and explain your system.

## extra  Is it pure?

Pure gold is made from gold atoms. Most of the gold we buy in shops is really a mixture of gold and copper because pure gold is very soft and is easily worn away.

The carat number tells you how much gold it contains. Pure gold is 24 carat. Most new jewellery is 9 carat. This means it contains 9/24 of gold, 9 carat gold is much harder than 24 carat gold.

**1** Look at the atom diagrams of gold and impure gold. Why do you think that 9 carat gold is harder than pure gold?

**2** Make a model to explain your ideas. You could use ping-pong balls or paper circles.

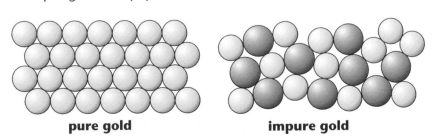

pure gold                 impure gold

# Making compounds

> ▶ The Space Shuttle uses hydrogen as a fuel. The hydrogen **burns** in oxygen to release energy. This energy makes the gases produced very hot. The gases expand rapidly and push the Space Shuttle forward. The Space Shuttle needs to carry enough hydrogen and oxygen for the outward and return journeys.

**1** What is made when hydrogen and oxygen react in the Shuttle?

In the Space Shuttle two elements combine to make a compound. This is a **chemical reaction**. A chemical reaction can be shown as a **word equation**.

hydrogen  +  oxygen  $\longrightarrow$  water

reactants  $\longrightarrow$  product

The  $\longrightarrow$  sign means makes.

You can identify a chemical reaction using the Chemical Clues.

## Chemical Clues

Chemical reactions:
◆ **produce completely new chemicals, not just a mixture of the starting chemicals**
◆ **cause a permanent change**
◆ **often involve changes in temperature.**

So, in the Shuttle:
◆ the new chemical produced is water
◆ we cannot easily change water back to hydrogen and oxygen
◆ the product made is a hot gas.

**2** List all the chemical reactions that you can think of that happen in your home. Use the Chemical Clues to make sure that they are all chemical reactions.

**3** Compare your list of reactions with the rest of your class. Are there any reactions that you didn't think of that other people did?

# Burning up

Coal is mostly carbon. When coal burns, the carbon reacts with oxygen in the air to make carbon dioxide. Smoke contains carbon dioxide. When something burns in oxygen we call it **combustion**.

The word equation for combustion is:
carbon + oxygen ⟶ carbon dioxide

**4** Why don't NASA use coal to power the Space Shuttle?

# Salt shaker

Sodium is a soft silvery metal. It is very reactive and reacts easily with water. Chlorine is a poisonous green gas. When sodium reacts with chlorine, the product is sodium chloride. Sodium chloride is ordinary table salt. You can add it to your food.

The word equation for making sodium chloride is:
sodium + chlorine ⟶ sodium chloride

> **WARNING:**
> Do not attempt this reaction. It is dangerous.
> Your teacher might demonstrate it for you.

# Flash bang!

> ◀ Magnesium burns quickly in oxygen once it is lit. Early flash bulbs used burning magnesium to give out a flash of white light.

Magnesium is a grey metal. Your teacher will burn some magnesium ribbon. When magnesium burns, it reacts with oxygen in the air to form magnesium oxide. Magnesium oxide is the white powder you see left. The reaction gives out bright white light.

The word equation is:
magnesium + oxygen ⟶ magnesium oxide

**5** Why could magnesium flash bulbs only be used once?

# Changing masses?

Early flash bulbs contained a mixture of magnesium and a chemical that would release oxygen. Manufacturers needed to mix the exact amounts of each chemical to react completely.

From the mass of magnesium and the formula of magnesium oxide, they could work out how much magnesium oxide they would make. They also knew that in a chemical reaction the mass of the reactants always equals the mass of the products. So they could work out how much oxygen they needed to release.

If a flash bulb contained 3 g of magnesium and made 5 g of magnesium oxide, how much oxygen did it contain?

magnesium + oxygen → magnesium oxide

$$3\,g + \text{mass of oxygen} = 5\,g$$
$$\text{mass of oxygen} = 5\,g - 3\,g = 2\,g$$

The bulb contained 2 g of oxygen.

Once the manufacturer knew how much oxygen they needed to release they could work out how much chemical to put into the flash.

**mass of reactants = mass of products**
reaction

6 Compare the properties of the reactants and the products in each of the chemical reactions on pages 96 and 97.

7 Write a word equation for the reaction of iron with sulphur.

8 Sugar is a compound. It is made from the elements carbon, hydrogen and oxygen. How are the properties of sugar different from the properties of the elements it contains? You may need to use other books to help you.

## extra  Why react?

In the Space Shuttle, hydrogen gas is mixed with oxygen gas and made to react. The molecules in both gases move because they have energy. The faster they move, the more energy they have. A chemical reaction will only happen when particles collide with enough energy to break up the molecules.

1 How could space technicians increase the number of collisions between hydrogen and oxygen molecules and so speed up the reaction in the Shuttle?

2 How can the Space Shuttle carry enough hydrogen and oxygen to fuel it on its journeys into space and back?

# Chemical change?

Chemical changes are very different to **reversible changes** such as melting or evaporating.

▶ The potter depends on chemical reactions in the kiln to produce the glazed finish on his pots.

◀ The farrier softens the iron by heating it, so that she can hammer it into shape. Once it is in the right shape the iron is cooled using water. These are reversible changes. The iron does not change chemically.

**9** Which of these are chemical and which are physical changes?

> ice melting    candle wax melting
> candle wax burning
> baking a cake    super glue setting
> burning an incense stick
> salt dissolving in water

**10** Make a table to show the differences between chemical and reversible changes.

## investigation

### Chemical change?

Carefully heat some copper carbonate, salol, zinc oxide, copper foil, paraffin wax, copper sulphate crystals and sand. Your teacher will show you how to heat each one safely.

Make a table to show your results. Add a column to your table to show if the changes are chemical changes or not. Use the Chemical Clues on page 96 to help you.

# ■ Oxidation

When an element reacts with oxygen, it is called **oxidation**. We say that the element is oxidised. Oxidations are some of the most common reactions in the world.

## A Space Problem

Although the Space Shuttle orbits the Earth outside our atmosphere, there is still some oxygen around. In the early Shuttle days, this oxygen reacted with the silver mesh on the solar cells and made flakes of silver oxide, as shown above. We have had to look for new protective coatings to use on the Shuttle solar panels.

The word equation for the reaction between silver and oxygen is:

silver  +  oxygen  →  silver oxide

1 Which other oxidation reactions have you met in this module?

## A Rusty Problem

Oxidation is also a problem for car manufacturers and owners. Most car bodies are made from iron. Iron is hard and strong and we can mould it to any shape we need. The problem with iron is that it reacts with oxygen in the air to make a type of iron oxide. We call it **rust**.

The word equation is:
iron  +  oxygen  →  iron oxide

2 How do car manufacturers stop cars from rusting?

# A Food Problem

Fats and oils, such as butter and olive oil, are all similar chemicals. When they go bad, it is because the fat or oil oxidises. The oils in fish oxidise very quickly. This makes the fish smell bad. Food manufacturers try to stop fats and oils in their foods from oxidising.

▲ Some foods, such as crisps and nuts, are packed in nitrogen gas. Nitrogen gas is harmless and if there is no oxygen the oil in the crisps cannot oxidise. The crisps stay fresher longer.

Other foods have chemicals added to stop oxidation. They are called **antioxidants** and they have E numbers. The most common antioxidants are E320 and E321.

3 Carry out a survey of foods to find out which contain antioxidants. Find the best way of organising your research results.

4 Do foods that don't contain fats or oils need antioxidants too? Use your research results to find out.

## Useful oxidations

▼ Oxidation can be useful too. It releases energy in our cells during **respiration**. Without this energy we wouldn't be able to do anything.

▼ When fuels, such as petrol, burn, they release energy to allow us to do things and have lots of fun! Burning fuels is a special sort of oxidation, called **combustion**.

### investigation

**An apple problem**

Apples turn brown when they are cut, because chemicals in the apple react with oxygen in the air. The oxide made is brown.

Plan an investigation to find out how you can stop apples browning.

5 Look back at your list of reactions from your home. Which reactions in your list are oxidation reactions? Which are useful oxidations are which are problem oxidations?

# Decomposition

We use lots of cement and mortar to build new homes. Cement and mortar are made from lime (calcium oxide). When limestone is heated at about 1 500 °C, it breaks down to make the lime we need.

The chemical name for limestone is calcium carbonate. When calcium carbonate is heated, it **decomposes** to make calcium oxide and carbon dioxide. Carbon dioxide is given off as a gas.

The word equation is:

$$\text{calcium carbonate} \xrightarrow{\text{heating}} \text{calcium oxide} + \text{carbon dioxide}$$

This type of chemical reaction is called **thermal decomposition**. 'Thermal' means that energy has to be added to heat the reactants before the reaction will happen.

6 Copper and zinc carbonate decompose when heated. Write word equations for their reactions.

## investigation

**Decompose it**

Plan an investigation to find which of the carbonates listed below decomposes the easiest. Can you put them in order, starting with the easiest?

- calcium carbonate
- copper carbonate
- zinc carbonate
- lead carbonate

# Displacement

▶ This nail is made from steel, which is mostly iron. It has been dipped in copper sulphate solution. Some of the iron atoms in the nail have **displaced** some of the copper atoms in the solution. The iron and the copper have swapped places. The displaced copper atoms have made a layer of copper on the nail. This is called a **displacement reaction**.

The equation is:
iron + copper sulphate ⟶ iron sulphate + copper

**7** Where can you find the iron sulphate made in the reaction between the nail and copper sulphate?

**8** Can you think of any other displacement reactions that you have seen during your science course?

---

## extra  *Backwards or forwards?*

Copper sulphate crystals are blue and they contain water. The water gives them their blue colour and their shape. When they are heated, they turn white and powdery and water is given off.

copper sulphate crystals $\longrightarrow$ copper sulphate powder + water
    (blue)                    (white)

If water is added to the white copper sulphate powder, it turns to blue copper sulphate crystals again. The reaction goes backwards and forwards. It is a real chemical reaction but it is also **reversible**.

The full reaction is written as:

copper sulphate crystals $\rightleftharpoons$ copper sulphate powder + water

This $\rightleftharpoons$ sign means that the reaction is reversible.

**1** How can this reaction be used to test for water?

**2** Work out a method for writing secret messages using your knowledge about copper sulphate.

---

- A single particle of an element is called an atom.

- An element only contains one type of atom.

- A compound contains two or more different atoms joined together.

- A compound always contains the same elements in the same proportions.

- A mixture may contain elements and/or compounds in any amounts.

- Chemical reactions make new substances and are not easily reversed.

- A chemical reaction can be written as a word equation.

- The mass of the reactants in a chemical reaction always equals the mass of the products.

- When an element combines with oxygen, an oxide is made. This is called an oxidation reaction.

- Many compounds break up when they are heated, these are thermal decomposition reactions.

- Some metals can displace others from a compound, these are displacement reactions.

**1** You have discovered a new element that is very expensive. What properties might it have to make it expensive?

**2** Copper sulphate powder has the formula $CuSO_4$. How many atoms of copper, sulphur and oxygen does one molecule of copper sulphate contain?

**3** Alcohol has the formula $C_2H_5OH$. How many atoms of carbon, hydrogen and oxygen does one molecule of alcohol contain?

**4** Write word equations for these reactions.

**a** hydrogen peroxide decomposes to give water and oxygen
**b** calcium reacts with oxygen to produce calcium oxide
**c** sodium reacts with water to produce sodium hydroxide and hydrogen gas
**d** aluminium reacts with oxygen to make aluminium oxide
**e** lead nitrate decomposes to give lead oxide, nitrogen dioxide and oxygen
**f** sulphur dioxide reacts with oxygen to make sulphur trioxide

**5** Which reactions in question 4 are oxidation reactions and which are thermal decomposition reactions?

**6** 12 g of carbon need 32 g of oxygen to react. How many grams of carbon dioxide are made?

**7** Divide these changes into chemical and non-chemical changes:

distilling sea water

igniting petrol in a car

cooking an egg

dissolving salt in water

sugar cane plants making sugar

taking a photograph

leaving fingerprints

using perfume on your skin

**8** Explain what we mean when we say that "chemical reactions are difficult to reverse".

Soap contains sodium stearate which cleans the skin. But, sodium stearate also reacts with some compounds dissolved in tap water, especially hard water. The product is scum which looks horrible. Manufacturers have to find ways to stop the scum forming, otherwise customers will not buy their products again.

**1** Investigate the reaction between soap and hard water.

**2** Find as many ways as you can to stop scum forming when soap is used in water.

# Stage lighting

▲ Rock bands use lighting to make their concerts really spectacular.

Lights can make a show exciting by creating special effects. However, with so many lights to control, lighting engineers need to use a computer to control them. The computer can can be programmed to produce a series of effects automatically.

▼ Shining light upwards throws strange shadows onto faces, making them look scary.

**1** How do you think lighting engineers create beams of coloured light to use as 'search lights' in concerts?

**2** The lights used to create special effects in concerts are big and heavy. How do you think lighting engineers manage to create all the different effects they need without moving heavy equipment during the concert?

**3** How can you make yourself look frightening by using lights in a dark room? Use torches to produce the light and see who can make themselves look the scariest.

Light

# ■ Moving light

Light travels quickly – almost a million times faster than sound does in air. No wonder that when there is a thunder and lightning storm, you see the lightning, and hear the thunder later. When light travels it carries energy with it – this is **radiation energy**.

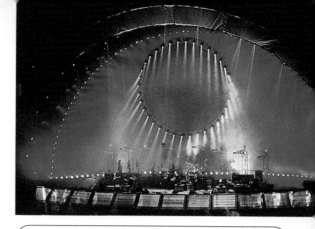

▲ Providing nothing gets in the way, light will travel in a straight line, forever!

## investigation

**From the stars**

Light spreads out as it moves away from it's **source**. Astronomers use the brightness of stars to work out how far away they are.

Carry out an investigation to find out how the brightness of a light varies with the distance from it. Try to describe a pattern in your data.

1 Navigators used to rely on accurate clocks to work out where their ship was. At one o'clock every day, this ball slid down the pole. Sailors on the Thames set their clocks by it. Why was this method used rather than firing a cannon or ringing a bell?

2 Astronomers use the 'light-year' as a measure of distances in space. Find out what a light-year is.

3 The light from the star Sirius takes 9 years to reach Earth.
**a** Is this because light travels slowly, or because Sirius is very far away? Explain your answer.
**b** Sound cannot travel through space. If it could, how long would sound take to reach us from Sirius?

# ■ Shadow games

When light hits an **opaque** object, the light is absorbed. The light that doesn't hit the object keeps moving until it hits a surface behind the object. A **shadow** forms on the surface, because the light has been blocked.

**Translucent** materials let light pass through. But they change the light's direction so you cannot see objects clearly through it. You can only see clearly through **transparent** materials.

4 Sort the items below into three groups: transparent, translucent and opaque materials.

> a bathroom window
> a bathing costume  curtains
> a light bulb
> a fluorescent light tube
> a milk bottle  a camera lens
> your eye-lid  space

## Large or small?

The size of a shadow depends on how far the light is from the object, and how far away the object is from the screen.

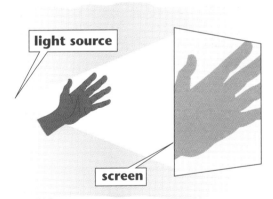

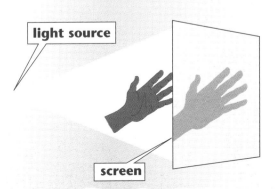

## Fuzzy shadows

The light from a big lamp will spread out from all of the lamp, not just the centre. So an object in the way of the light will stop some of the light from reaching the surface behind it, but not all of it. This means that the shadow will have fuzzy edges. Shadows formed using sunlight aren't sharp because the Sun is large.

A shadow will have sharp edges if the light source is very small, or if the object is very close to the surface behind it.

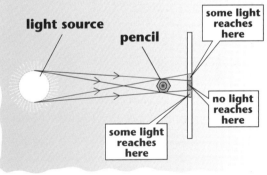

5 How can Yun make her hand shadows really sharp?

**6**

These shadows are made by flat metal puppets. They are used in Indonesia.

**a** Draw a diagram to show how you think the source of light, the puppets and the screen are set up.

**b** Why aren't the shadows really sharp, even though the edges of the puppet are?

**c** How could a small puppet be used to make a very large shadow?

**7** To read the time from a sundial you have to see where the shadow is pointing. Why is it impossible to measure the time really accurately using a sundial?

---

## investigation

### Picture perfect

A pin-hole camera is made from a light-proof box with a small pin-hole in one end. The pin-hole is so small that only light travelling in one direction can get through to the film at the back. This means that you can get a clear picture on the film.

Make your own pin-hole camera.

Carry out tests to find out how to get the clearest picture.

---

## extra  *In the dark room*

Photographs have to be developed in rooms which are lit only by dim red light. It is important to keep normal light out because the film would be ruined. However, people need to be able to enter and leave the dark room easily. Many photographers create an entrance that is designed to keep the light out, but allows people to walk in.

**1** Design a dark room to make sure that no light can enter. You will need to stop light entering through the windows and doors.

**2** Suggest why the sides of the entrance to a dark room are usually painted matt black.

# ■ Reflecting light

When light hits a shiny surface, such as a mirror, the light bounces back. It is just like a ball bouncing off a wall. We call this effect **reflection**. However, unlike the ball, light does not slow down each time it bounces, although some of it may be absorbed. This means that light can be reflected millions of times without it stopping.

Metals are used in jewellery because they are good reflectors. Glass and water can reflect light, but they also allow some of the light to pass through them. Polished surfaces and some plastics also reflect light.

◀ A lake can act just like a mirror if the water is still. The light reflects off the lake producing an image of the surroundings.

1 You are stranded on a hillside and want to reflect sunlight to someone in the valley below so that they can get help. What might you be carrying that would make a good reflector?

## Rules of reflection

When light reflects from a flat surface, the angle the light hits the surface at is the same as the angle at which it bounces off. These two angles are called the **angle of incidence** (i) and the **angle of reflection** (r).

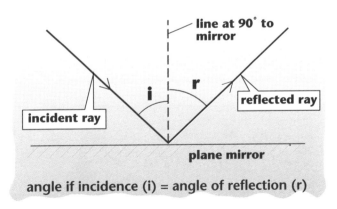

angle if incidence (i) = angle of reflection (r)

Look at your reflection in a flat mirror (called a **plane mirror**), the image looks just like you. However, your right side appears to be on your left and your left side appears to be on the right. You seem to be back to front. All mirror images are like this, we say that they are **laterally inverted**.

### *investigation*

**Reflectors**

Carry out an investigation to prove that the angle of reflection is always the same as the angle of incidence when light reflects from a plane mirror.

# ■ Bending light

> ▶ When you look at pencils through a glass of water they look very strange. This is because the light reflected from the pencils changed direction as it passed through the glass and water.

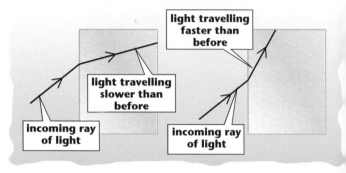

Whenever light moves at an angle from one material into another, it changes direction. This effect is called **refraction**.

Refraction happens because light travels at different speeds in different materials. If the light slows down when it moves into a new material, it refracts one way. If it travels faster than before, it refracts the other way. The larger the change in speed, the more the direction of the light changes.

light travelling faster than before

light travelling slower than before

incoming ray of light

incoming ray of light

> ▶ Light travels faster in hot air than in cool air. On a hot day, the air close to the ground gets hot, while air higher up stays cool. Because of this, light coming down from the sky can be refracted back up. A traveller looking at the ground can see the sky, just as if it were reflected in water – although the light has actually been refracted, not reflected. This is a mirage.

where fish appears to be

where the fish is

> ◀ This fish seems to be higher in the pond than it really is. This happens because light reflected from the bottom refracts as it passes from the water into the air. Your brain tells you that the fish is higher in the pond than it really is because the 'seeing' part of your brain doesn't understand refraction.

**2** Why might a mirage be a problem to a traveller in a desert?

**3** Why could refraction be dangerous to a diver?

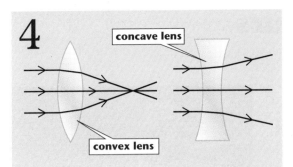

4

These lenses change the direction of the light by refraction. Make a list of the jobs we use lenses for. Which type of lens would you use for each of the jobs you have listed?

## investigation

### Diamonds are forever?

Design an investigation to test whether a diamond is real or glass. You can't use chemical tests because diamonds are too expensive, but you could use refraction. Use the data below to help you.

| Material | Refractive index compared to air (air =1.0) |
| --- | --- |
| glass | 1.62 to 1.69 |
| diamond | 2.41 |

## extra  Internal reflection and optical fibres

If light hits a surface at a very small angle, the light reflects back into the first substance. It doesn't refract. This effect is called **total internal reflection**.

In 1965 George Hockman and Charles Kao showed that it was possible to send data along thin fibres of glass using pulses of light that were internally reflected along the fibre. The technology became known as **fibre-optics**. However, the glass they used was not very pure, and the light only travelled a metre before it was absorbed.

By 1977, researchers had developed purer glass and the world's first fibre-optic system was set up between Stevenage and Hitchin. It carried 2000 signals on one fibre. Today, one fibre can carry 30000 conversations. The signals travel for over 50 km before they need amplifying.

1 What was the main cause of delay between 'inventing' the fibre-optic system, and putting it into practice?

2 Bundles of fibre-optics are used by doctors to examine inside patients.
**a** Why are fibres used to carry light into the patient, rather than just putting a small lamp inside the patient?
**b** Why are fibres used to transmit pictures from inside a patient, rather than placing a small camera inside. The pictures are not as clear, so why is the system used?

3 Why is it important not to have sharp bends in an optical fibre?

4 Satellites and cellular phones use radio signals.
**a** What is the advantage of a mobile phone over one linked by fibre-optics?
**b** Suggest reasons why fibre-optic systems are likely to remain the main way of transmitting phone messages.

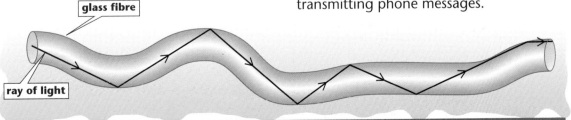

# ■ Rainbow of colours

▶ White light is made from all the colours of the rainbow mixed together. When white light is split up by a prism we can see a **spectrum** of the colours of the rainbow.

We know that white light is made from a mixture of coloured light because we can separate white light into all the different colours by passing it through a glass prism. We say that the light is **dispersed** by the prism.

The light is dispersed because different **wavelengths** of light are refracted by different amounts by the glass. The different wavelengths make the light different colours. Longer wavelength light appears red, and shorter wavelength light appears violet.

▲ longer wavelength = less energy carried = red
shorter wavelength = more energy carried = violet

## *investigation*

### Make a spectrum

Shine a beam of white light through a prism to make your own spectrum. Draw what your spectrum looks like, showing all the different colours of light.

Now try to make your spectrum combine again to make white light.

**1** What are the different colours of light that combine to make white light?

**2** Some people use the sentence 'Richard Of York Gave Battle In Vain' to help them remember the order of the colours in a spectrum. Make up your own sentence to help you remember.

# Making colours

## Filtering

▼ White light can be used to make coloured light by using coloured filters to absorb unwanted colours of light. These blue filters absorb all of the light except the blue light. It has not *changed* the light from white to blue, but only the blue light can pass through. A red filter works in exactly the same way.

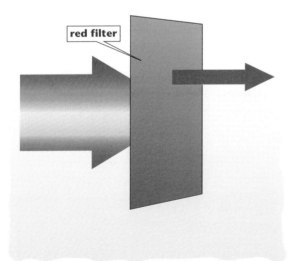

red filter

3 Do you think that dark or pale filters heat up most when they are used? Explain your answer.

4 Green filters only allow green light to pass through. Why would it be dangerous for car drivers to use sunglasses with green lenses?

## Pure colours

▲ Lasers produce light of a single wavelength.

Lasers produce light of one wavelength and therefore of a single, pure colour. They can produce very thin beams of light but the total amount of light is small. Lasers cannot be used to light a stage, although they can produce impressive effects.

## Adding Colours

Any colour of light can be made by mixing red, green and blue light in different amounts. Television screens use dots which release red, green or blue light. Combinations of these three can make other colours.

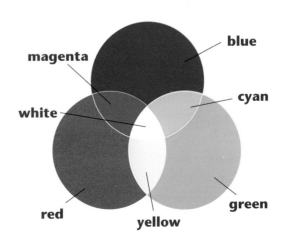

blue

magenta

cyan

white

red

yellow

green

## False colour

the person sees a red object because it has not absorbed the red light

▶ An object appears coloured because it absorbs the other colours of light.

▲ The colour of an object depends upon which colours of light it reflects. A red candle reflects red light but absorbs all the rest.

▲ A candle will look very different in different coloured light. If there is no red light, there is no way that the candle can reflect red light, so it will appear to be black.

**5** Street lamps give out mainly yellow light. One night the police receive a report that a black car has been involved in an accident.
**a** What colour might the car appear under white light?
**b** What difference would it make if the report had said that the car was yellow?

**6** In horseracing, each jockey wears different colours to make them easy to recognise at a distance. At an evening meeting, someone suggests lighting the racetrack with blue light to make it more exciting. What problems might this cause and who will be affected most?

## investigation

### What is colour?

Investigate the effect the colour of light has on the appearance of different coloured objects. How will you make the light different colours?

Present your data in a table that can be used by lighting engineers and costume designers so that they can easily tell what different costumes will look like under different lights.

# How do your eyes work?

Your eyes are amazing things. They let you see things which are near or far and in many directions. You can see in 4 million colours and can quickly adjust to different light levels. Your eyes even clean themselves!

We see everything around us because of the light coming from objects. Some objects emit light (these are called **luminous** objects) but most objects just reflect light that has come from another source.

1 Group the items in the box into two groups, those that emit light and those that reflect it.

> you    this page
>
> the image on a television screen
>
> lightning    the Sun
>
> the image on a cinema screen
>
> a star    a flame
>
> a light bulb switched off

2 List as many things as possible that can go wrong with eyes. Describe how we try to help people with these problems.

3 You blink so often that your eyes are closed for ¹/₂ hour during each day while you are still awake. Why do you blink so often?

## investigation

### Who's eyes are best?

Design an investigation to test the claim that brown eyed people can 'see better' than blue eyed people.

What sort of data would you gather?

How would you handle the data to draw your conclusions?

# ■ Your eye

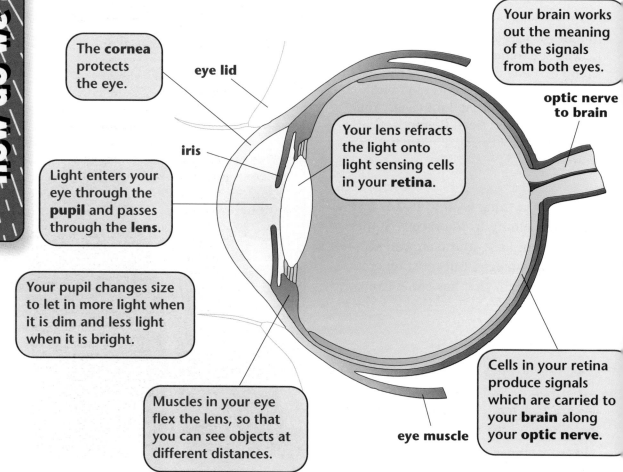

The **cornea** protects the eye.

eye lid

Your brain works out the meaning of the signals from both eyes.

optic nerve to brain

iris

Your lens refracts the light onto light sensing cells in your **retina**.

Light enters your eye through the **pupil** and passes through the **lens**.

Your pupil changes size to let in more light when it is dim and less light when it is bright.

Muscles in your eye flex the lens, so that you can see objects at different distances.

eye muscle

Cells in your retina produce signals which are carried to your **brain** along your **optic nerve**.

**4** Which part of your eye does each of these jobs:

**a** adjusts to cope with different light levels

**b** adjusts to focus on objects different distances away

**c** allows you to detect coloured images

**d** allows you to detect black and white images.

**5** Some blind people regain their sight by having a 'cornea transplant'. The blind person's cornea is cut out, and is replaced by one taken from a donor – perhaps a road accident victim. Where is the cornea in your eye, and what is its job?

**6** The lens of your eye makes an image at the back of your eye. This image is upside down but you don't see things upside down. Why?

## extra  *Animal vision*

Many organisms can detect light. Detecting light lets them hunt for food and escape from predators.

Predators usually have eyes at the front of their head. This allows them to judge distances accurately. Herbivores usually have their eyes at the side of their head. This gives them much greater 'all round' vision so that they can spot predators coming near.

1  An eagle can see finer detail than a human because it has more light sensing cells in its retina. The cells are also closer together. How is this useful for the survival of the eagle?

2  In what ways have humans been successful animals because of their excellent eyesight.

3  Imagine that you could buy eyes in a shop. Write an advert for human eyes. Which features could you stress to a potential customer?

▲ This woodlouse has no eyes, but it can still find a dark place. Why is that useful to the woodlouse?

▼ This bee can detect colours with its eyes. It can also see shapes. How does it use this ability?

- Sight is one of your senses.
- Light travels at a steady speed in a straight line.
- Light travels much faster than sound.
- We can see light sources because light from them enters our eyes
- We can see non-luminous objects because light reflects from them and enters our eyes.
- Shadows form when opaque objects absorb light, but other light passes around the object.
- Light is reflected from surfaces such as mirrors or polished metals.
- Light can be internally reflected.
- Light can be refracted as it passes through a material.
- White light can be dispersed into a range of colours by refraction.
- Filters are used to absorb colours from white light, leaving only light of a specific colour.
- Coloured objects appear differently in white and coloured light.

117

**1** The larger points on the diagram show the colours available from one lamp. How many are available?

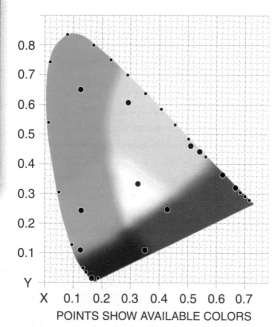

POINTS SHOW AVAILABLE COLORS

What colour light will the lamp produce when the colour mix is:

**a** Y = 0.1, X = 0.2
**b** Y = 0.4, X = 0.4
**c** Y = 0.3, X = 0.6

**2** What colour will a red object appear when a lamp produces these colours?

**a** red  **b** green
**c** blue  **d** white

**3** Smoke can be used to create different lighting effects. Is this because smoke is translucent, transparent or opaque?

**4** If it wasn't for the cooling fans, the colour filters on the big stage lamps would get very hot. Why?

**5** To direct the beam of light, the whole lamp could be moved. However, the designers decided to use a moveable mirror instead. Why?

**6** To make the light from a lamp appear red, a red filter is placed in front of it. A member of the band says they want it an even deeper shade of red and that you should put another layer of the red filter over it, "to turn it even more red". How would you reply?

**7** Some stage lamps contain several metal disks which can be placed in front of lights to make specially shaped shadows onto the stage. These disks are called 'gobos'. Look at the gobos below and suggest the effect each one can be used to create.

○ Choose an interesting photograph from a magazine or book. It could be a photograph of a live concert, a play or just a picture of someone interesting. Draw a plan of the stage of photo-set for your photograph and suggest where the light would have been placed to get the lighting effect.

○ Work out what coloured filters might have been used?

# Are acids always harmful?

We use acids in many different ways. Many foods naturally contain acids. Milk contains lactic acid. Oranges and lemons contain citric acid. Processed foods often have acids added during their manufacture. Phosphoric acid is one of the ingredients in my favourite drink, Coca Cola.

**330ml**
**SOFT DRINK**
**WITH VEGETABLE**
**EXTRACTS**

INGREDIENTS:
CARBONATED WATER, SUGAR,
COLOUR (CARAMEL E 150d),
PHOSPHORIC ACID,
FLAVOURINGS, CAFFEINE.

**BEST SERVED - ICE COLD**

BEST BEFORE END-
see base of can for date

**1** Use Universal Indicator paper to find out the pH of a range of drinks. You might try tea, coffee, squash, carbonated water, fruit juice, milk and canned drinks.

**2** Which ingredients do you think make the drinks acidic or alkaline?

**3** What do acid foods and drinks do to your teeth?

**4** Produce a leaflet to show primary school children how they can stop acids from damaging their teeth.

Reactions of Acids

119

# ■ All about pH

pH is a measure of how acid or alkaline a solution is. Solutions of acids have a pH below 7 and solutions of alkalis have pH values over 7.

You can measure pH using **Universal Indicator**. This turns different colours to show different pH values.

1 Make your own Universal Indicator chart and add labels to show the pH of the drinks you have tested.

There are many different indicators. The first indicators used were plant dyes. Litmus is a purple solution made from lichen. It turns red with acids and blue with alkalis. Universal Indicator contains a mixture of solutions to give different colours at different pHs.

---

## *investigation*

### Natural indicators

The purple colour from red cabbage leaves is a natural indicator. Find the best way to extract the purple colour from red cabbage. Investigate how the colour changes when it is mixed with an acid or an alkali.
Investigate using other plant colours as indicators. You could try blackberries, sloes, beetroot or blackcurrants.

---

2 Blue hydrangeas grow in acid soil. If the soil is neutral or alkaline, the flowers turn pink. Can you explain why? Why might this fact be useful if you were a gardener?

**pH**

| strong | 1 |
| | 2 |
| acid | 3 |
| | 4 |
| | 5 |
| weak | 6 |
| neutral | 7 |
| weak | 8 |
| | 9 |
| | 10 |
| alkali | 11 |
| | 12 |
| | 13 |
| strong | 14 |

# Weak or strong?

Acids taste sour and they are dangerous. You eat some acids every day, but these acids don't make holes in your tongue. They are **weak acids**.

> ▶ Vinegar contains ethanoic acid.
> Apples contain malic acid.
> Most fruit and vegetables contain ascorbic acid, better known as vitamin C.

**3** Look at some of the foods you eat every week. Make a list of all the different acids you eat in a week.

> ▶ In 1947, a business man, John Haigh, was arrested for murder. He thought that he couldn't be found guilty of murder if there was no body, so he had dissolved his victim in sulphuric acid ($H_2SO_4$). No trace of the body was ever found. His idea didn't work. He was found guilty of murder and was hanged in Wandsworth Prison on 6 August 1949.

Sulphuric acid, nitric acid and hydrochloric acid are **strong acids** – they would definitely make holes in your tongue if you ate them!

Acids and alkalis, especially the strong ones used in laboratories, are dangerous. You must never touch them unless told to do so by your teacher.

**4** Which elements make a molecule of sulphuric acid? How many atoms of each element are there?

**121**

**5** A difference of one on the pH scale means that the substance is ten times more/less acidic or alkaline than the substance with the next pH. For example an acid with pH 2 is ten times stronger than an acid with pH 3.

**a** How many times more alkaline is pH 10 to pH 8?

**b** How many times more acidic is pH 1 to pH 4?

## Acid strength

Acid strength is different to how strong or weak an acid is; it is a measure of how much acid a solution contains, not how strong the actual acid is.

A solution with a lot of acid dissolved in water is called a **concentrated** acid. A solution containing a small amount of acid dissolved in water is called a **dilute** acid.

## extra What make an acid strong?

All acids contain hydrogen. In a weak acid, most of this hydrogen stays joined to the rest of the acid molecule. In a strong acid, most of the hydrogen separates from the rest of the acid molecule and becomes free hydrogen **ions**. But note, not all molecules containing hydrogen are acids.

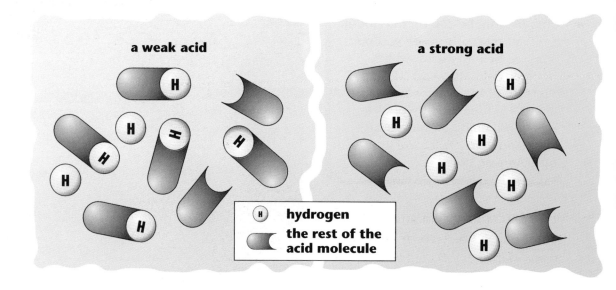

a weak acid · a strong acid

H hydrogen

the rest of the acid molecule

**1** Draw a similar diagram to show a medium strength acid.

**2** Which acid has the lower pH value, a strong acid or a weak acid?

**3** Can you think of a reason why all acids have to be dissolved in water?

**4** Test some citric acid crystals with Universal Indicator paper. Now dissolve some crystals in water and test with indicator paper again.
Repeat the tests using tartaric acid crystals.

**a** What does this tell you?

**b** Can you explain your results?

# A stomach problem

It may surprise you to learn that your stomach contains hydrochloric acid and is pH 2.
The acid in your stomach disinfects your food. Sometimes your stomach makes too much acid and this gives you **indigestion**.

Medicines to cure indigestion contain substances, such as magnesium hydroxide, that cancel out the extra acid. The products formed in your stomach are a **salt** and some water, which are both neutral.

A substance that reacts with an acid to make a salt and water is called a **base**. An alkali is a just a base that can dissolve in water.
When a acid reacts with a base it is called a **neutralisation reaction**:

acid + base/alkali ⟶ salt + water

---

### investigation

**Acid guts**

Your teacher will give you some stomach acid. Use indigestion medicines to investigate what happens in your stomach when you take an indigestion medicine or pill.

---

# About salts

When you use the word salt, you usually mean the table salt that you put on your food. Its chemical name is sodium chloride and its formula is NaCl.

To a scientist, salts are a family of chemicals made from acids. All acids contain hydrogen. If you replace the hydrogen with a metal, you make a **salt**.

1. What gas do you think would be given off when hydrochloric acid reacted with sodium?

2. What salt would you make if you replaced the hydrogen in hydrochloric acid with zinc?

▲ Copper sulphate solution is used to kill pests on plants.

▶ Gunpowder, for fireworks, is made from potassium nitrate.

Different acids make different types of salts. The last name of the salt comes from the acid. It is its surname. The metal gives the acid its first name.

| Some salts | | |
|---|---|---|
| **Acid** (formula) | **Its salt name** | **Example** (formula) |
| hydrochloric (HCl) | chloride | sodium chloride (NaCl) |
| sulphuric ($H_2SO_4$) | sulphate | copper sulphate ($CuSO_4$) |
| nitric ($HNO_3$) | nitrate | potassium nitrate ($KNO_3$) |

3 Which acids made these salts:

a zinc nitrate
b magnesium sulphate
c copper chloride
d lead nitrate?

4 Which salts would you make from:

a hydrochloric acid and calcium
b sulphuric acid and zinc
c nitric acid and magnesium
d sulphuric acid and aluminium?

# Salty solutions

The design on this metal plate is made by dissolving parts of the plate in acid. First I dip the plate in wax, then scratch my design into it. The plate then goes into an acid bath and the acid eats away the exposed metal.

My plants grow best at pH 7. The problem is that my soil is very acidic. I am adding lime, which is calcium oxide, to the soil to help neutralise it.

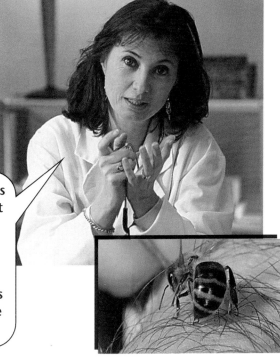

Wasp stings are very painful. The wasp injects alkali under the skin. The easiest way to treat a wasp sting is to rub an acid, such as vinegar, into it as soon as possible.

Bee stings are also painful. The bee injects acid under the skin. Calamine lotion contains zinc carbonate and can be used to neutralise the acid sting and take the pain away.

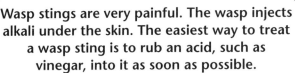

All these people are making salts by replacing the hydrogen in an acid with a metal. The student is using a metal to replace the hydrogen. The farmer is using the metal calcium in calcium oxide to replace the hydrogen. The doctor is using the metal in an alkali to replace the hydrogen. The zinc in zinc carbonate replaces the hydrogen in the acid bee sting.

**Acid + metal?**

Not all metals can replace the hydrogen from acids. Plan an investigation to find out which metals and acids you can use to make salts.

*Note:* Do not use sodium, potassium, lithium or calcium.

## What's made?

When a salt is made using a metal and an acid, hydrogen gas is given off. This type of reaction is an example of a **displacement reaction**. The general pattern is:

metal  +  acid  $\longrightarrow$  salt  +  hydrogen

When a salt is made using a metal oxide and an acid, the displaced hydrogen joins with the oxygen from the metal oxide to make water. The general pattern is:

metal oxide  +  acid  $\longrightarrow$  salt  +  water

**5** Write a general pattern for making a salt from:
**a** a metal hydroxide and an acid
**b** a metal carbonate and an acid
(metal hydroxides contain metal, oxygen and hydrogen atoms and metal carbonates contain metal, carbon and oxygen atoms).

**6** What would you expect to see when zinc is added to dilute sulphuric acid?

**7** What would you expect to see when sodium carbonate is added to dilute hydrochloric acid?

**8** Write word equations to show which acids and metals you would use to make:
**a** magnesium chloride
**b** zinc nitrate
**c** aluminium sulphate
**d** iron nitrate
**e** zinc chloride.

**pH changes**

Investigate how the pH changes when sodium hydroxide is added to hydrochloric acid. Produce a graph from your results.

# ■ Acid rain

► This lake in Sweden used to contain a large variety of plant and animal life, but now it's one big acid bath. Many fish have died and those that remain cannot breed. The water is one hundred times more acid than it should be and cannot be drunk anymore. They are trying to neutralise the acid by dropping lime (calcium oxide) into the lake. The lime neutralises the acid.

The Swedish people blame Britain for making the rain acidic. Fossil fuels, such as coal and oil, are made from carbon and hydrogen just like other plant and animal material. British coal also contains 1.6 % sulphur. These substances in the air make the rain acidic.

| What happens | The chemistry | The effect |
|---|---|---|
| fossil fuel burns | carbon + oxygen ⟶ carbon dioxide<br>sulphur + oxygen ⟶ sulphur dioxide | air pollution |
| petrol used in car engines | nitrogen + oxygen ⟶ nitrogen oxides | |
| oxides plus water make acid rain | carbon dioxide + water ⟶ carbonic acid<br>sulphur dioxide + water ⟶ sulphuric acid<br>nitrogen oxides + water ⟶ nitrogen acids | rain becomes acidic |
| acid rain falls over Sweden | | plants are affected |
| metals like aluminium dissolve in acid rain and are washed into lakes and rivers | | lakes become acidic, water life starts to die |

1  Can you explain why rain is more acid on the east coast of Britain than the west coast?

# Chemical Weathering

▲ This statue is made from limestone. Acid rain has reacted with the limestone to make a salt, carbon dioxide and water. The new salt is washed away by the rain and so the limestone wears away.

▲ Acid rain would dissolve the metal in this bridge. It must be painted to keep the acid rain away from the metal.

Chalk, limestone and marble are all made from calcium carbonate. When an acid is added to these rocks, they fizz as carbon dioxide gas is given off and the rock is worn away.

Rain water is a weak acid, over thousands of years it has reacted with limestone wearing away the rock to make caves and potholes. During the last 100 years, rain water has become more acidic and the process has speeded up.

2 Why has rain water become more acidic in the last century? Why is this a problem?

3 Write a word equation to explain what happens as calcium carbonate rocks are chemically weathered.

## investigation

### Acid effects

Investigate the effect of acid rain on different materials. Use laboratory acids (which are stronger than acid rain) to speed up your investigation.

# How Acid?

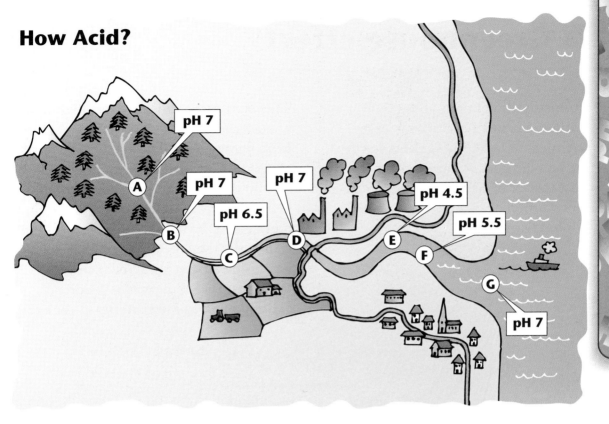

Organism survival at different pHs

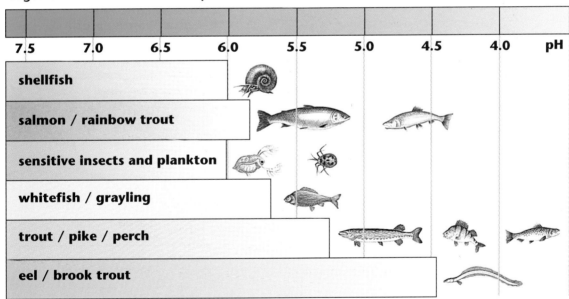

> ▲ Most plants and animals survive best in environments with a neutral pH. Acid rain may have a pH as low as 2.4.

**4** What happens to the acidity of the river from its source to the sea?

**5** Why do you think the pH drops at E and F? What makes it return to neutral at G?

**6** Which animals would you expect to find at C, D, E and F?

# ■ Greenhouse effect

Air naturally contains about 0.03 % carbon dioxide, but burning large amounts of fossil fuels releases extra carbon dioxide. Some scientists think that this extra carbon dioxide is causing our world to warm up, this is called **global warming**.

The extra carbon dioxide acts like a greenhouse around the Earth trapping extra energy from the Sun. We call this effect the **Greenhouse Effect** and carbon dioxide is a 'greenhouse gas'. Carbon dioxide, water vapour and methane in the air all trap energy, but it is only the level of carbon dioxide that is increasing so quickly. Other scientists think that the extra carbon dioxide is causing our weather patterns to change.

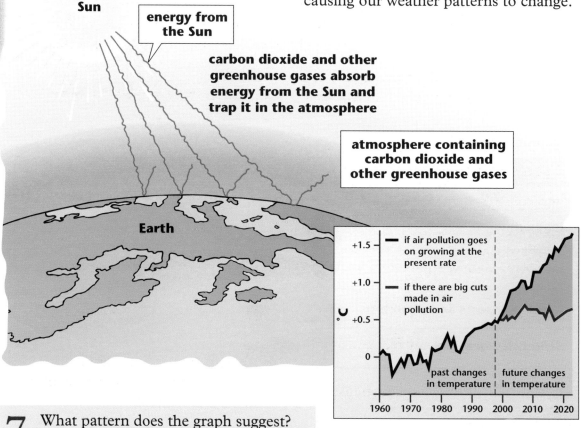

Sun

energy from the Sun

carbon dioxide and other greenhouse gases absorb energy from the Sun and trap it in the atmosphere

atmosphere containing carbon dioxide and other greenhouse gases

Earth

— if air pollution goes on growing at the present rate

— if there are big cuts made in air pollution

°C

+1.5
+1.0
+0.5
0

past changes in temperature | future changes in temperature

1960  1970  1980  1990  2000  2010  2020

**7** What pattern does the graph suggest? By how much has the temperature risen since 1960?

**8** How can we make the big cuts in air pollution that are needed?

**9** The world's leaders met in New York in June 1997 to discuss plans to cut the increasing levels of greenhouse gases. What suggestions would you make?

**10** Without the natural greenhouse gases, the Earth would be 30 °C colder.
**a** What are the natural greenhouse gases?
**b** What difference do you think natural greenhouse gases make to life on Earth?

## extra *Climate changes*

Our climate has always changed. In the past, Britain has been covered in ice during Ice Ages and has had tropical weather at other times. No-one can be absolutely sure that increasing carbon dioxide levels cause global warming.

---

The Greenhouse Effect is a theory.
Before you can say it is a true fact, you need evidence.
You collect your evidence by making observations.

---

One way that scientists work is:

They see a problem.

They think up a theory to explain the problem.

Lots of scientists collect evidence and carry out experiments to test the theory.

If the evidence backs up the theory, it becomes accepted as a true fact.

**1** What else could cause changes in our weather?

**2** What sort of observations do scientists need to make in order to decide whether the Greenhouse Effect theory is a true fact?

**3** What is the difference between a theory and a fact?

---

**Key ideas**

- pH is a measure of how acid or alkali a solution is.

- Acids have a tart taste and a pH less than 7.

- Alkalis have a soapy feel and a pH greater than 7.

- An alkali is a base that can dissolve in water.

- Indicators show acidity/alkalinity by changing colour.

- A concentrated acid has more acid molecules in solution than a dilute acid.

- A metal and an acid react to give a salt and hydrogen.

- A metal oxide/hydroxide and an acid react to give a salt and water.

- A metal carbonate and an acid react to give a salt, water and carbon dioxide.

- An acid can be neutralised by adding an exact amount of alkali to make a neutral salt.

- When fossil fuels are burnt, carbon dioxide and sulphur impurities make rain water acid. Acid rain damages materials and living organisms.

- Burning fossil fuels releases extra carbon dioxide into the air. This is thought to create global warming by the Greenhouse Effect.

**1** Make an instruction chart for 11-year-olds about the safe handling of acids.

**2** What makes a good indicator?

**3** A cook shredded and cooked some red cabbage and then stirred in some cider vinegar. The cabbage changed from red to blue as the vinegar was added.

Explain what happened using the words in the box.

> pH   indicator   acid   neutral

**4** Which hydroxide and acid would you use to make sodium chloride? Write a word equation.

**5** Finish these word equations:

zinc + sulphuric acid →
magnesium oxide + hydrochloric acid →
sodium carbonate + sulphuric acid →
lead oxide + nitric acid →
calcium carbonate + hydrochloric acid →
sodium hydroxide + nitric acid →

**6** What is the difference between a strong acid and a concentrated acid?

**7** Baking powder makes cakes rise. It contains tartaric acid and sodium hydrogen carbonate. How does baking powder work?

**8** Which are bases? Which are alkalis?

| Name | Is it soluble? |
| --- | --- |
| copper oxide | no |
| sodium carbonate | yes |
| potassium hydroxide | yes |
| magnesium oxide | no |
| calcium hydroxide | slightly |

**9** Write a magazine article describing the effects of acid rain on our environment.

**10** What effects does global warming have on life on Earth? Why do you think that it is important to reduce global warming? Draw a poster or give a presentation to your class about your thoughts and findings.

- Many foods and drinks like Coca Cola are acidic.
- Make a list of materials that are used to package acidic foods and drinks.
- What properties do these materials need to have?
- Plan and carry out an investigation to find out which materials are best for packaging acidic foods and drinks.

# ■ Picking a winner

▲ ▶ Which of these animals would you pick to win a race? Which would be best to carry a load up a steep, stony track?

People breed horses to do particular jobs – carrying heavy loads, running fast, or jumping well. Winning racehorses are valuable because they are used to breed more racehorses. Owners believe that if a horse is fast it could pass on this useful feature to its foals. Donkeys are used to do tough jobs because they are strong and can survive harsher conditions than horses.

**1** Racehorses and donkeys have been bred from the same ancestors. How do you think racehorses and donkeys became so different?

**2** Make a list of features you could use to tell one racehorse from another.

**3** Make a list of features that you think a racehorse may pass on to its foals.

**4** Carthorses look more like racehorses than donkeys do. Describe the main differences between a carthorse and a racehorse. Do you think that a carthorse could become a racehorse with training?

**Variation**

# ■ Spot the difference

> ► You need to look carefully to see the differences between these two kittens.

These two kittens look alike, but they do have features that we can use to tell them apart. We could measure the distance between their ears or the number and length of their whiskers. If we had the kittens in front of us we could measure mass, body or tail length and height and we could look for coat markings and scars.

**1** Examine these woodlice carefully. Make two lists, one of their similarities and one of their differences.

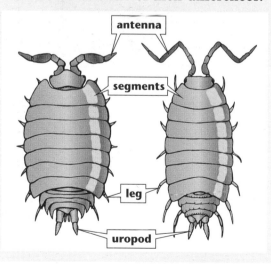

antenna

segments

leg

uropod

## How do humans vary?

People are easy to tell apart because we have so many differences. Some differences are obvious, for example, we are either male or female, not something in-between. Differences where there are a limited number of options are **discontinuous variations**.

Other differences can vary much more, such as height, body mass or hair colour. People can be short, tall or anywhere in-between. We say that these are **continuous variations**.

### 𝒊𝒏𝒗𝒆𝒔𝒕𝒊𝒈𝒂𝒕𝒊𝒐𝒏

**Differences**

In groups, collect data on height, eye colour, hand span and ear lobe shape for everyone in your class. Decide what the best way to display each set of data is. Present your data to the rest of your class.

2 Look at each of your data sets. Do they show continuous or discontinuous variation?

3 For each of your class data sets decide whether it is a feature that might be passed on to children. Are any of these features affected by the way you have grown up?

4 The Parents Association in your school is planning to raise funds by selling school sweatshirts. How would you find out how many sweatshirts in each size they will need to order?

## ■ Do differences matter?

Animals and plants have differences that can help them to survive in their **environment**. These differences help organisms **adapt** to their environment. They may help them to:

♦ avoid being eaten
♦ find a partner for **reproduction**
♦ get food and water
♦ find shelter, space and anything else that they need.

▲ Piranahs are fierce fish that hunt smaller fish.

▲ Polar bears hunt seals across the ice sheets in the Arctic.

▲ Cacti live in hot dry deserts.

5 Explain, in as much detail as you can, how each of the organisms shown above is adapted to live in its environment.

6 Choose one of the environments in the box below. Find out how organisms in your chosen environment are adapted to live there. Draw a poster to show your findings.

| desert | oak woodland | sea shore | deep sea bed |
| --- | --- | --- | --- |
| waste land | mountain | pond | |

# Peppered moths

The dark peppered moth first appeared in the middle of the Nineteenth Century in the new industrial cities of the north-west. By the start of the Twentieth Century, light moths were rare in the cities, but were still common in the country. Scientists came up with three possible reasons for this change:

◆ Industrial cities were smoky and this blocked out most of the sunshine. Moths need to warm up in the sunshine before they can fly, feed and reproduce. The dark moths absorbed more warmth and so could feed and reproduce better.

◆ The smoke and soot were taken in by caterpillars and moths. The light moths were poisoned but the dark moths could survive the pollution better.

◆ Dark moths resting on sooty trees were better camouflaged than light moths and so were less likely to be eaten by birds.

▲ There are two types of peppered moth: a light one and a dark one. Peppered moths rest on the trunks of birch trees with their wings open.

## investigation

**Testing ideas**

Design an investigation to test whether dark-coloured moth shapes warm up faster than light-coloured moth shapes.

**7** Which reason for the appearance of the dark moths do you think is correct? Explain why.

**8** Use your library to find out what the real reason for the appearance of dark moths was.

## extra Extinction

Organisms can be perfectly adapted to their environment. When an environment changes, the organisms living there must adapt or they will become **extinct**.

In New Zealand, flightless birds, such as the kiwi, adapted to live and breed on the ground because there were no **predators**. In the Nineteenth Century Europeans started living on the islands. They brought rats with them from their ships and later cats to kill the rats. The rats and cats then escaped into the wild.

**1** What effect do you think the arrival of rats and cats has had on the kiwis?

**2** Can you find any more examples of how humans have brought other species to extinction or close to it.

**3** Do you think that we are still affecting organisms in this way as we explore the world?

**4** Produce a leaflet to show tourists how they could travel without damaging the wildlife in an area.

# How are features inherited?

> Kirk and Michael Douglas are actors. But they share faces as well as jobs. Michael has **inherited** his father's chin, face shape and eyes. How did Michael come to share these physical features with his father?

Everyone starts as an **ovum** which is **fertilised** by a single **sperm**. The ovum came from the mother and the sperm from the father. Ova and sperm pass on information from parents to their children. When a sperm meets an ovum only the **nucleus** of a sperm enters, so information about inherited features must be in the nucleus.

1 What is fertilisation?

2 Where is inherited information carried in sperm and ova?

## What's in the nucleus?

> A cell's nucleus carries large amounts of a chemical called **DNA**. When a cell divides to make new cells you can see the DNA coiled into **chromosomes** in the nucleus. Ordinary human cells have 23 pairs of chromosomes. These chromosomes have been coloured to make them stand out.

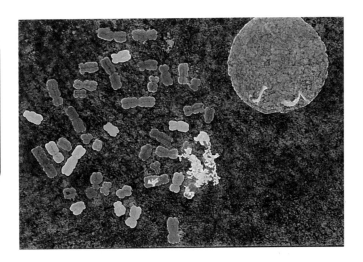

**DNA** carries instructions on how to build an organism following a pattern. DNA carries information about every part of a organism from the chemicals in cell membranes, to the exact shape of someone's ear lobes or colour of hair. A set of DNA instructions for making one tiny part of a person is called a **gene**. One **chromosome** carries enough genes for thousands of human parts. When new cells are made they inherit an exact copy of the DNA.

3 What is a chromosome?

4 How many chromosomes are there in an ordinary human cell?

5 In your own words, explain what a gene is.

**137**

# Ovum meets sperm

Sperm and ova are different from all other cells. They only get a copy of one of the chromosomes in each pair. So sperm and ova carry half of the genes for the parent's body.

▶ When a sperm fertilises an ovum the two sets of chromosomes combine so that there is now a complete set of DNA instructions for a new human.

The developing child gets half its genes from each parent, so the child has a mixture of mum's and dad's features. Each child in a family inherits a slightly different combination of chromosomes, and so has a slightly different combination of features, they look alike but they are not the same.

6 How is the DNA in a sperm different to the DNA in other body cells?

7 Explain how a child can have its mother's nose but its father's eye colour?

## Boy or girl?

There is one unusual pair of chromosomes. These are the **sex chromosomes**. A person carrying two X chromosomes is female, but a person with one X and a Y chromosome is male. A woman can only pass on the X chromosome to her eggs, but a man can pass on an X or a Y chromosome into a sperm.

8 Explain why it is the father who determines which sex a baby will be.

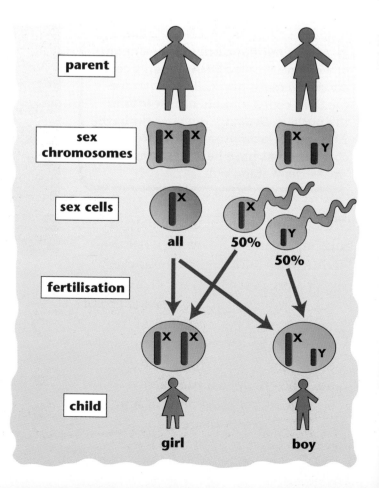

parent

sex chromosomes

X X

X Y

sex cells

X

X

Y

all

50%

50%

fertilisation

X X

X Y

child

girl

boy

# Twins

▶ Non-identical twins are the result of two ova, each fertilised by a sperm, developing at the same time. Like any other brothers and sisters they will inherit different mixes of their parents features.

◀ Identical twins have the same genes. A single fertilised ovum develops and then splits into two groups of cells. Each group of cells develops into a baby. Each baby has the same set of genes and the twins will have the same mixture of features from their parents.

**9** Why are identical twins identical?

**10** From what you understand about twins, try to explain how identical triplets might develop.

Because identical twins inherit identical sets of genes, scientists have used them to research ideas about how our environment affects the way we are. The environment we live in affects us all, but when you study identical twins you always have something to compare the effect to.

Identical twins who spend most of their life together will probably end up looking and behaving alike. However, twins will not always grow up exactly alike, especially if they do not have the same life experiences. So, if one twin has a passion for sport they might develop much bigger muscles than their twin. Twins separated as young children will often grow up to be very different.

**11** Do you think that continuous or discontinuous features more likely to be affected by your environment?

## Do your genes match?

Although a gene carries the information for a single body part you actually have two genes for each body part; one gene on each of a pair of chromosomes. The instructions in the two genes may be identical or slightly different.

Some versions of genes dominate any other version. This is a **dominant gene**.

The other gene does not show up, and is called a **recessive gene**. Even though the recessive gene is not active it is still there, and can be passed on to any children.

Eye colour is determined by your genes. Brown eye genes dominate blue eye genes. If a person has a brown eye gene, their eyes will be brown no matter what gene is on the other chromosome.

### Inheriting eye colour

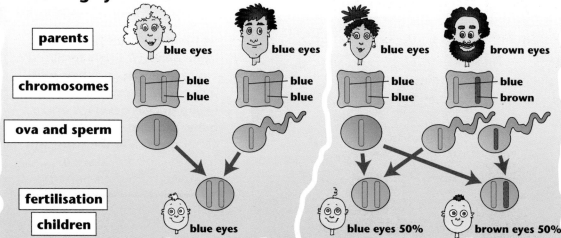

| parents | | |
|---|---|---|
| chromosomes | | |
| ova and sperm | | |
| fertilisation | | |
| children | | |

parents: blue eyes — blue eyes — blue eyes — brown eyes

chromosomes: blue/blue — blue/blue — blue/blue — blue/brown

children: blue eyes — blue eyes 50% — brown eyes 50%

**1** Red hair colour is inherited in a similar way to blue eyes. Can you work out how a couple with dark hair could have a red-headed baby?

**2** Read the information sheet about cystic fibrosis. Imagine that you are a magazine agony aunt. A reader is worried about having children as her husband's sister's son has just been diagnosed as having cystic fibrosis. Write a reply explaining why someone with two normal genes married to a carrier is unlikely to have children with cystic fibrosis.

# ■ Improving organisms

Farmers try to produce more food from the same land by using better varieties of plants and more productive animals. Farmers use varieties of wheat that have short, strong stems to withstand summer storms and cows that produce lots of milk. These varieties are the result of **selective breeding**.

Farmers have always kept good animals for breeding. They did not know about genes, but they knew that good features are often passed on to the next generation. By breeding parents with useful features, varieties developed that were suited to the local environment. These are the varieties we farm today.

▲ Wild sheep live on mountains. They have a thick coat of coarse hair over a layer of woolly fibres to keep them warm in cold, windy environments.

▲ Merino sheep have been bred so that they have no coarse hairs in their coats. Their coats make very soft and fine wool.

## Keeping good features

Good plants are valuable, but when one plant fertilises another the seeds will carry a mixture of genes from each parent. When the seeds grow they will not be the same as either parent. They may not have such nice flowers or strong stems or sweet fruit or they could be better.

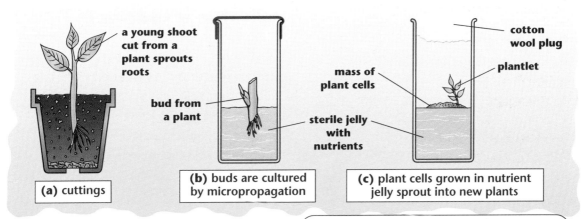

a young shoot cut from a plant sprouts roots

bud from a plant

mass of plant cells

sterile jelly with nutrients

cotton wool plug

plantlet

(a) cuttings

(b) buds are cultured by micropropagation

(c) plant cells grown in nutrient jelly sprout into new plants

▲ Gardeners can grow lots of new plants from a single good plant to build up a stock of identical plants. This is called **propagation**.

### *investigation*

#### Make it grow

Gardeners can use rooting powder to help cuttings sprout roots.

Design an investigation to find out the best strength of powder to use for rooting geranium cuttings.

How will you make your test fair?

12 Draw a flow chart to show how your class could grow a large number of geraniums to raise funds in the school summer fete.

13 In East Anglia the soil is dry and cold winds pick up salt as they blow across the North Sea. There are few hedges to act as windbreaks. If you were choosing a wheat variety to grow, what three features would you want your chosen variety to possess?

14 Explain what is meant by selective breeding.

# Sorting into groups

> ▶ Each llama in a herd is different. But, there are even more differences between llamas and other members of their **family**, the camels. All the members of the camel family share some features that are not found in other two toed animals.

Grouping together organisms which share features is called **classification**. Living organisms have been divided into five **kingdoms**.

The five kingdoms are:
◆ the animal kingdom (all animals)
◆ the plant kingdom (all plants)
◆ the monera (bacteria)
◆ the protista (other single-celled organisms)
◆ the fungi (mushrooms, yeast, etc.)

In a kingdom all the organisms share a few important features. For example, all the organisms with a **nervous system** are grouped in the animal kingdom. Jellyfish and chimpanzees are animals because they both have a nervous system. However, they do not have much else in common. So, the members of a kingdom are sub-divided into smaller and smaller groups which have more features in common.

1 Why do you think that classifying living organisms is important?

2 Viruses are not included in any of the five kingdoms. From what you know about viruses can you think why?

## What is a species?

A **species** is the smallest classification group. Members of a species are like each other and can breed together to produce young like themselves. They cannot breed successfully with members of another species.

▲ Horses and donkeys are very similar but they are different species. When a horse and a donkey mate they produce a mule, like the one above. A mule is like neither parent and cannot breed.

## Names

We give names to the organisms around us, such as the Spotted Flycatcher or Hair Grass. But the same organism can have different names in different parts of the world. Classification is important because it lets scientists give organisms names that can be recognised all over the world, the names also carry a lot of information about the organism.

The two-part Latin names used by scientists are like our own names. Maria Jones belongs to the Jones family and she is called Maria. The first part of a Latin name is shared with other close relatives. The second part of a Latin name tells us which member of the group it is. This name is often based on a feature of the animal.

| Latin name | Common name | Description |
|---|---|---|
| Apis mellifera | honey bee | mellifera is Latin for honey |
| Dynastes hercules | hercules beetle | a giant beetle, named after a strong man |
| Micromys minutus | harvest mouse | minutis is Latin for tiny |
| Eryngium maritimum | sea holly | maritimum is Latin for connected with the sea |

## ■ Animals galore

Animals can be split into two main groups: **invertebrates** (animals without a backbone) and **vertebrates** (animals with a backbone).

Invertebrates have no backbone but they do have nerves. Invertebrates are divided into seven main groups to make them easier to identify.

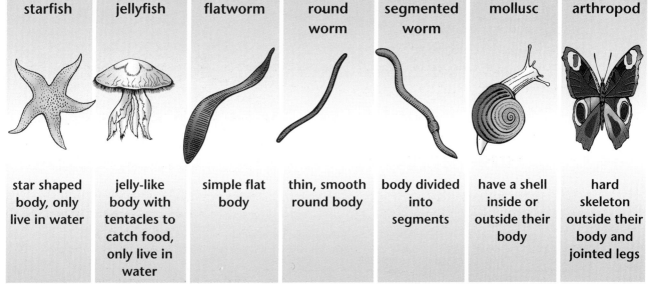

| starfish | jellyfish | flatworm | round worm | segmented worm | mollusc | arthropod |
|---|---|---|---|---|---|---|
| star shaped body, only live in water | jelly-like body with tentacles to catch food, only live in water | simple flat body | thin, smooth round body | body divided into segments | have a shell inside or outside their body | hard skeleton outside their body and jointed legs |

## Arthropods

**Arthropods** are the most important invertebrate group because there are more of them than all the other animal groups put together. Arthropods have a hard outside skeleton, a body made of segments and limbs with joints.

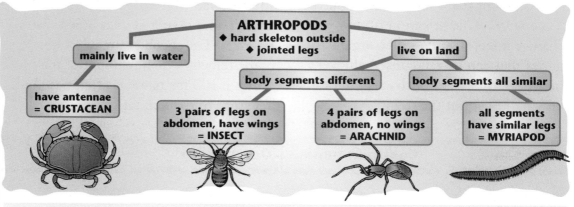

3 Which of the organisms in the box are insects?

| woodlouse  bee  ant  ladybird  fly  butterfly |
| :---: |
| spider  centipede  greenfly  dragonfly  wasp |
| flea  daddy-long-legs (crane fly)  grasshopper |

## Vertebrates

Vertebrates have a skeleton inside their body, a nerve cord running inside their backbone, and a tail. Land vertebrates usually have four limbs, water vertebrates have fins instead.

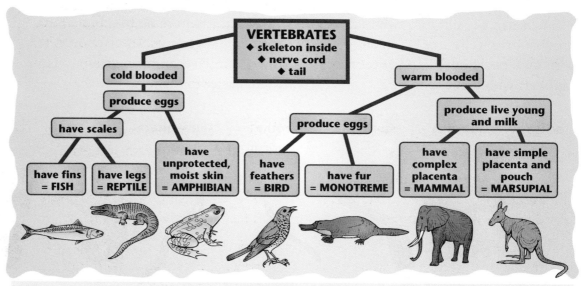

4 The animals in the box are different to most other members of their groups. Explain how each one differs giving as much detail as you can.

| eel  ostrich  penguin  snake |
| :---: |

5 Humans should have a tail, can you find out what has happened to our tails?

# Sorting plants

Plants use **chlorophyll** to trap light energy and produce glucose during **photosynthesis**. Their cells are surrounded by a **cell wall**.

People often think that **fungi** are plants, but they are not. They do not have any of the plant features. They are, in fact, a completely separate kingdom.

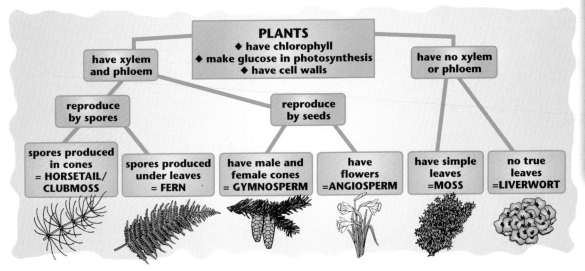

**PLANTS**
◆ have chlorophyll
◆ make glucose in photosynthesis
◆ have cell walls

have xylem and phloem

have no xylem or phloem

reproduce by spores

reproduce by seeds

spores produced in cones = HORSETAIL/ CLUBMOSS

spores produced under leaves = FERN

have male and female cones = GYMNOSPERM

have flowers =ANGIOSPERM

have simple leaves =MOSS

no true leaves =LIVERWORT

## investigation

### Key design

Produce a **biological key** that will help you to classify plants into the six groups shown above. Does your key work? Try it out on some friends to see if they can use it.

6 Use your key to divide these trees into gymnosperms and angiosperms. You might need reference books to help you.

| oak | cedar | horse chesnut | scots pine |
| sycamore | yew | spruce | willow | larch |

- There are differences between the individuals in a species.

- Some features only allow a few variations, such as sex. These are discontinuous variations.

- Other features allow a continuous range of variations. These are continuous variations.

- Variations in an individual may affect its chances of living and breeding successfully.

- Features are carried as genes on chromosomes in the nucleus.

- Genes are passed from parent to child through sperm and ova.

- Farmers chose animals and plants with good features to breed from. This is selective breeding.

- Selective breeding results in new types of organisms suited for a particular purpose.

- Propagation is used to produce large numbers of identical plants.

- Differences between organisms are used to classify them.

1 Danielle and Jade carried out a survey of garden snails.
They searched for snails in their gardens on three separate warm evenings after a short rain shower. They:
◆ measured the diameter of each snail shell
◆ counted how many brown bands ran around the snail shell.
After they had measured a snail they put a small dot of pale nail varnish under the shell before they let it go.

These are their results.

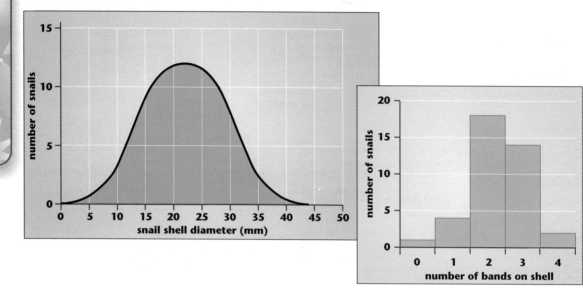

a Why did Danielle and Jade carry out their survey on warm, wet evenings?
b Why did they survey on three different evenings?
c Why did they mark the snails after they had been measured?
d Look at the graphs. Do the measurements show continuous or discontinuous variation?

2 Jade noticed that the snails in the short grass in the park on the way to school did not have bands, or only had very light bands, but the snails in Danielle's vegetable garden and shrubs had clear, dark bands. Can you think of three reasons for this difference?

3 Explain how selective breeding has led to the development of racehorses and carthorses.

Investigate

1 Survey the snails in your garden, your school grounds or a local park. Record shell diameter, the number of bands and the direction of the coil viewed from the top. Collect together the data from your group. Decide the best way to present your data about shell size and number of bands.

Are your results similar to Danielle and Jade's? Is there a link between the size of snails and the number of bands?

2 Snails are thought to have a sense of 'home' and will return to the same place each evening. How could Jade and Danielle investigate whether this was true or not using their data?

# Glossary

**acid** A solution with a pH below 7.

**acid rain** Rain that falls with a pH below 7 because of pollutants in the air.

**adaptation** A characteristic that can affect the survival of an organism in its environment.

**adolescence** Changing from a child into an adult, also called puberty.

**alkali** A soluble base that forms a solution with a pH above 7.

**antioxidants** Chemicals added to foods to stop oils and fats oxidising.

**arthropods** The group of organisms that have jointed legs and a hard skeleton outside their bodies

**asteroid** A piece of rock, orbiting the Sun.

**atom** The tiny particles that all matter is made from.

**birth** The time when a baby leaves its mother's uterus.

**bud** Part of a plant that can grow into a new shoot.

**cell** The building blocks that all organisms are made from.

**cell membrane** The bag that surrounds a cell and holds everything inside. The membrane also sorts out what materials can and cannot enter the cell.

**chemical change** Also called a chemical reaction. A change where the products are different to the starting chemicals.

**chemical formula** A way of showing a material based upon the chemical symbols of the atoms it is made from.

**chemical symbol** The symbols given to each element so that they can be recognised throughout the world.

**chlorophyll** The green pigment that traps sunlight energy in leaves.

**chloroplast** Structures found only in plant cells that contain chlorophyll to trap sunlight energy for photosynthesis.

**chromosome** Coils of DNA found in all cell nuclei that carry the information needed to make an organism.

**classification** Sorting organisms (or rocks) into related groups.

**cochlea** Part of the inner ear where sound waves are changed into electrical signals to go to the brain.

**combustion** Burning in air, a form of oxidation.

**comet** A large lump of rock and ice which comes from the edge of the Solar System, and gets hotter as it gets nearer to the Sun forming a tail of water vapour.

**compound** Two or more elements chemically joined together.

**conduction** The transfer of heat through solids.

**conductor** Any material that lets heat flow through it easily.

**conservation of energy** The law that says that energy is never created or destroyed, it just transfers and is dissipated.

**consolidation** The formation of sedimentary rock by layers of sediment building up and squashing the layers below.

**constant composition** The law that states that however a compound was made, its formula will always be the same.

**continuous variation** Variations where there is an unlimited range of possibilities.

**convection** The transfer of heat through liquids and gases by currents.

**core (Earth)** The very centre of the Earth.

**crust (Earth)** The outer layer of the Earth.

**crystals** Solids where the particles are arranged in regular patterns.

**cytoplasm** The jelly-like substance that forms most of a cell.

**decomposition** A reaction where one substance breaks down into two or more different substances.

**deposition** Sediments drop out of a stream of water, forming layers of sediment which may later be turned into sedimentary rock.

**discontinuous variation** Variations where there are only a few distinct possibilities.

**dispersion** Plants spreading their seeds away from the parent plant.

**displacement** A reaction where an element displaces another from a compound.

**Dissipation** The spreading out of energy as it transfers.

**DNA** The substance that carries all our genetic information.

**dominant gene** A gene that will always show as a characteristic, whatever other different genes for that characteristic are present.

**eardrum** The membrane that changes sound waves into the movement of

**echo** The reflection of a noise from a hard surface.

**energy efficiency** The percentage of useful energy that you can get out of a machine.

**elastic potential energy** All stretched or squashed materials have elastic potential energy.

**electricity** Energy that is carried around a circuit by an electrical current.

**electrons** The charged particles found in metals that are responsible for the conduction of electricity and heat.

**element** A substance made from only one type of atom.

**ellipse** The shape or the orbit of the planets around the Sun, it is like an oval.

**embryo** The first two months of a new babies life in its mother's uterus.

**energy** The ability to do something (work).

**energy transfer device** Any object that transfers energy, e.g. a motor car.

**environment** The area in which an organism lives.

**erosion** The wearing away of rock by particles of rock carried by the wind or water.

**Eustachian tube** The tube that connects your ears to your nose.

**evaporation** Changing state from liquid to gas at a temperature lower than the boiling point.

**extinction** The dying out of all the members of a species.

**fertilisation** When male and female nuclei fuse to create a complete set of instructions for a new organism.

**fetus** A baby forming in its mother's uterus when cells start to specialised to do particular jobs, about two months after fertilisation.

**fibre-optic** A very thin glass tube down which light can travel due to total internal reflection, to carry information.

**flower** The reproductive part of a flowering plant.

**food chain** A food chain shows what an organism eats and what it is eaten by.

**fossil** The remains of an ancient organism that have been turned to stone.

**frequency** The number of waves that pass a point in any second. Frequency is measured in Hertz (Hz).

**fruit** The wall of the ovary after the ovules have been fertilised, the ovary wall can be fleshy like a plum, or hard like a nut.

**gene** Part of a chromosome that carries the information for one tiny part of an organism.

**germination** When a seed starts to grow into a plant.

**global warming** The warming of the Earth thought to be caused by increases in the greenhouse effect.

**glucose** The sugar made during photosynthesis.

**gravitational potential energy** All objects above the ground have gravitational potential energy.

**gravity** The force of attraction between two objects.

**greenhouse effect** The trapping of sunlight energy in the Earth's atmosphere by gases which warms the Earth. More greenhouse gases in the atmosphere are thought to be making the Earth warmer.

**guard cells** The cells that open and close stomata.

**hormone** Chemical messengers that travel around the body in the blood

**humus** Material from dead plants and animals that makes up part of the soil.

**hypothermia** Being dangerously cold.

**igneous rock** Rock made from cooling molten rock (magma).

**indicator** A substance that shows whether a solution is an acid or alkali by a colour change.

**inheritance** Passing on genetic information from adult to offspring.

**insulator** Any material that does not easily let heat flow through it.

**internal energy** The kinetic energy contained within an object, often called its 'heat'.

**invertebrates** Animals that do not have a backbone.

**kinetic energy** The energy of movement. All moving objects have kinetic energy.

**lava** Molten rock (magma) from a volcano.

**leaf mosaic** The pattern leaves make so that they trap as much sunlight as possible.

**light** Radiation energy.

**luminous** Something that gives out light.

**lunar eclipse** A eclipse of the Moon, the Earth moves between the Sun and Moon so that the Moon is in the Earth's shadow and cannot be seen.

**machine** A device used to do work.

**magma** Molten rock, from the Earth's mantle and core.

**mantle (Earth)** The liquid part of the Earth under the crust.

**mass** The amount of matter that an object is made of, measured in kg.

**menstrual cycle** The monthly cycle of the thickening of the uterus lining, releasing of an ovum and the release of the uterus lining during a 'period'.

**metamorphic rock** Rocks formed when other rocks are heated and/or squashed in the Earth's crust.

**meteor** A lump of rock that enters the Earth's atmosphere and gets destroyed.

**meteorite** A lump of rock from space which reaches the ground.

**microgravity** Where the force of gravity is very small.

**mineral** A natural substance (an element or a compound). Rocks are made from mixtures of elements.

**mixture** Two or more elements or compounds that are not chemically joined together.

**molecule** Two or more atoms chemically joined together, the atoms could be the same or different.

**Moon** The only natural satellite orbiting the Earth.

**Moon phases** The changing views of the Moon as it orbits the Earth every 28 days.

**nucleus** The control centre of a cell.

**orbit** The path an object follows as it moves around another object.

**ore** A rock that contains a useful mineral.

**ovary** Part of the female reproductive system where female sex cells (ova in animals and ovules in plants) develop.

**ovulation** The release of an ovum from the ovaries of a woman.

**ovule** The female sex cell of a plant.

**ovum** The female sex cell of an animal.

**oxidation** A reaction where a substance combines with oxygen.

**palisade cells** Cells in the upper part of a leaf packed with chloroplasts to trap sunlight.

**penis** Part of the male reproductive system, used to put sperm inside a woman's vagina.

**period (menstruation)** Part of the menstrual cycle where the uterus lining leaves the body through the vagina

**pH** A measure of the acidity or alkalinity of a liquid or solution of a solid.

**photosynthesis** The process by which plants make food (glucose) from trapped sunlight.

**pitch** How high or low a note is. A high note has a high pitch.

**placenta** The organ in the uterus that provides food and oxygen to the embryo/fetus and takes away waste products from the embryo/fetus.

**planet** A large object made of a mixture of gas, liquid and solid moving round the Sun.

**pollen** The grains that hold the male sex cells in plants.

**pollination** Transfer of pollen from the anther of one flower to the stigma of another.

**potential energy** Stored energy in an object.

**predator** An animal that eats other animals.

**propagation** Growing more plants from one plant using cuttings or micropropagation.

**puberty** Changing from a child into an adult, also called adolescence.

**radiation** An electromagnetic wave that warms things up.

**reflect** When light or sound bounces back off an object.

**refraction** When light is bent as it passes through a transparent object.

**respiration** Releasing energy in cells through a chemical reaction.

**root hair cells** Cells near the tip of a root that have hair-like extensions to absorb water.

**salt** The compound made when a metal displaces hydrogen from an acid.

**satellite** An object that orbits something else. The Moon is a natural satellite of Earth. TV satellites are artificial satellites.

**secondary sexual characteristics** Changes to your body that happen at puberty.

**sediment** Particles that settle out from a suspension.

**sedimentary rock** Rocks made when sediments are squashed and stick together.

**seed** The fertilised ovule from a plant that contains the embryo plant and the food stores needed for germination.

**selective breeding** Breeding your best animals or plants together to try to produce offspring with a mixture of the characteristics you want.

**sex chromosomes** The chromosomes that make you male or female.

**sexual intercourse** The process of getting sperm inside a woman so that they can fertilise an ovum.

**shadows** Dark patches make on a surface when an object stops light getting to the surface.

**soil** A mixture of weathered rock particles and matter from dead plants and animals.

**solar eclipse** A eclipse of the Sun, the Moon moves between the Sun and Earth so that the Moon makes a shadow on Earth and the Sun cannot be seen.

**Solar System** The complete collection of asteroids, planets and comets moving around the Sun.

**sound wave** 'Squeezes and stretches' of particles made by an object vibrating. Sound waves carry kinetic energy.

**specialised** Adapted to do a particular job.

**species** A grouping of organisms. Organisms of the same species can breed together, organism of different species cannot breed together successfully.

**spectrum** All the colours of light in white light spread out so that they can be seen.

**sperm** A male sex cell of an animal.

**sperm tube** The tube that leads from the testes, through the penis and to the outside down which sperm travel.

**stamen** The male parts of a flower (the anther and filament).

**stigma** The sticky female part of a flower where pollen lands.

**stomata** Holes found in the surfaces of leaves, mostly on the underside, used for gas exchange.

**Sun** A very large amount of hot gas, releasing enough energy to produce light. It is our nearest star.

**testis** The part of the male reproductive system where sperm are produced.

**thermal conductivity** The measurement of how quickly energy travels through a material.

**thermal decomposition** A reaction where one substance breaks down into two substances when it is heated.

**transparent** A material that lets light pass through.

**umbilical cord** The structure that joins an embryo/fetus to the placenta.

**uterus** The part of the female reproductive system where a baby can develop.

**vacuole** A structure found in plant cells, they store water and help to keep the plant rigid.

**vacuum** A space where there are no particles of matter.

**vagina** The opening to the female reproductive system from the outside.

**vertebrate** An animal that has a backbone.

**vibrate** Small backwards and forwards movements.

**volcano** A site where magma from the Earth's mantle breaks through the crust.

**weathering** Breaking down rocks by physical and chemical changes.

**work** Transferring energy.

# ■ Index

Index